Gluten-Free Cookbook for Beginners

Gluten-Free
COOKBOOK FOR
Beginners

100 Essential Recipes to Go Gluten-Free

Jessica Kirk

Photographs by Marija Vidal

**ROCKRIDGE
PRESS**

For general information on our other products and services or to obtain technical support, please contact our Customer Care Department within the United States at (866) 744-2665, or outside the United States at (510) 253-0500.

Rockridge Press publishes its books in a variety of electronic and print formats. Some content that appears in print may not be available in electronic books, and vice versa.

Interior and Cover Designer: Diana Haas
Art Producer: Sara Feinstein
Editor: Gurvinder Singh Gandu
Photography © 2020 Marija Vidal. Food styling by Victoria Woollard.
Title Page: Photography by Marija Vidal

ISBN: Print 978-1-64876-504-9 | eBook 978-1-64739-593-3

R0

This book is dedicated to my father,
who taught me that life is good, and to my mother,
who taught me to simply trust in Him.

Contents

Introduction

Hi, friend. I'm Jess Kirk, the author of this cookbook that you're currently holding. I'm an interesting combination of a veterinarian by day and food blogger by night. I've run my website, BlessHerHeartYall.com, a gluten-free comfort foods recipe website, for the past six years and recently published my first cookbook, *Gluten-Free Comfort Foods*. I know how hard and overwhelming it can be to start creating gluten-free dishes at home because I was in your shoes a little over a decade ago. I have celiac disease and have been eating strictly gluten-free since the day my doctor diagnosed me. I don't have much of an option; I must make sure that gluten isn't a part of my life.

No matter what brought you here—whether you're like me and you don't have any choice, you have found out you have a gluten sensitivity and need to watch your gluten intake, or you are just curious about what gluten-free cooking and the gluten-free diet could offer you—this book can help you find answers, solutions, and really, really good recipes.

With every journey there is a hero who must overcome. One of the most common issues I hear from readers cooking gluten-free for the first time is the quantity of specialty gluten-free products needed to create those drool-worthy gluten-free recipes, but fear not: this couldn't be further from the truth. There is absolutely no need to go out and buy an exorbitant number of gluten-free products to produce amazing gluten-free dishes. I'll show you which gluten-free products should be staples in your pantry and which ones you can put back on that grocery store shelf. I like to feel like the hero of my kitchen by saving money and pantry shelf space, and I am sure you wouldn't mind that, either.

Another issue I hear about from beginners is the crumbly and hard gluten-free baked goods that they thought would be soft, moist, and fluffy. I've been that cook before, and I don't want you to have that same experience. I'll show you how to create those pillowy, soft, fluffy baked goods that taste just like the original gluten-containing recipes do. There will be no disappointed faces in your kitchen.

After explaining all you need to know about gluten and cooking with gluten-free ingredients, I'll showcase different recipes from breakfast and brunch favorites to the most commonly asked-for snacks and appetizers, the soups and sides you crave but can't touch, the meatless mains you wouldn't think would rock without gluten, and the best desserts you don't want to miss. Of course, I couldn't skimp on my favorite type of food to cook: main courses. They are so easy to make and insanely delicious to devour. And because sometimes the secret is in the sauce, I've also included a chapter on my favorite staple dips, sauces, and dressings to take simple dishes to the next level.

I have written this book for the people just starting on their gluten-free adventure. The recipes and other content in this book are easy to follow and the last thing from intimidating. I hope that you find both the inspiration and the confidence to cook gluten-free dishes as well as find some go-to recipes that you love, that your family asks for week after week, and that find their way into your daydreams. Cooking without gluten doesn't have to be scary or hard; you just need the basic framework to get started. Let me guide you through easy gluten-free recipes, one simple favorite at a time. I will help you be that gluten-free recipe hero, delicious win after delicious win!

CHAPTER 1

Gluten-Free 101

This chapter will give you all the information that you need about living a gluten-free lifestyle. I'll cover everything from defining what gluten is and what it means to be gluten-free to shopping tips and other essential information to get you started.

Defining Gluten-Free

You've probably heard the terms "gluten" and "gluten-free" for some time now, and perhaps curiosity has gotten the best of you. Maybe that's why you picked up this book. If you're trying to decide whether to go gluten-free or not, it's probably best to start by learning what gluten really is.

Gluten is a protein found in cereal grains like wheat, barley, and rye. It is used in many foods as a binder to maintain the correct shape, rise, and consistency of the product. Gluten keeps baked goods fluffy, moist, soft, and elastic (think of it as the glue that holds it all together). It is a big part of why a chewy chocolate chip cookie, a soft loaf of bread, and an al dente pasta are perfectly soft and bouncy and hold their shape. Gluten is found in many common cooking products, such as all-purpose flour, premade sauces, spice mixes, and even sometimes hidden in processed meats.

Going Gluten-Free

Practicing a gluten-free lifestyle essentially means avoiding any products that contain gluten. You'll eat foods that may be naturally gluten-free or foods that are reimagined with gluten-free ingredients, such as a soft, spongy cupcake. Going gluten-free will mean something different to everyone. It may mean eating just one gluten-free meal. It may mean being gluten-free for one day, or it may mean gluten-free for a lifetime. It depends on where you are in your gluten-free journey and what you want to get out of it. For example, you may simply have a personal preference for avoiding gluten; you may have an intolerance or sensitivity to gluten; or you may, like me, have a medical reason for avoiding gluten. Because you have picked up this beginner-friendly book, I think we should start simple. Let's be gluten-free for one recipe and build from there.

Gluten-Free FAQs

It's completely normal to have questions when you're beginning something new. To make things easier for you, I've listed some of the more commonly asked questions

Managing Celiac Disease with a Gluten-Free Diet

Being diagnosed with the autoimmune disease known as celiac disease, or even a gluten sensitivity, usually comes with some sort of sticker shock. I was incredibly nervous when I was finally diagnosed and yet relieved to finally know what was going on with me. A diagnosis might be the reason why you picked up this book. I know from experience that the start of a gluten-free diet is by far the hardest part of the journey. It gets easier from there.

With a gluten sensitivity or other diagnosis that requires you to avoid gluten, you must use extreme caution not to use any gluten-containing products or cross-contaminate surfaces or cooking utensils to avoid potential health issues. This might sound scary, but really, it isn't so hard. The easiest way to maintain a gluten-free lifestyle is to not buy or keep gluten-containing products in your home (I'll talk more about this in chapter 2). This way, you will be much less likely to come into contact with gluten and therefore much less likely to trigger a gluten reaction. If you have any specific questions or concerns regarding your particular diagnosis and diet, don't hesitate to reach out to your health care professional.

I receive about the gluten-free lifestyle. If you have any additional concerns, you should reach out to a medical professional or dietitian for personalized guidance.

» **Will I miss out on important nutrition with a gluten-free diet?** Absolutely not. Gluten-free foods do away with gluten; however, they do keep all the nutrition of the dish. Gluten itself has no nutritional value, so you won't miss anything on that end.

» **Will my energy level decrease without gluten?** I've never felt tired or sluggish because of my diet and have not heard anyone in the plethora of gluten-free groups I am a part of complain about this, either. In fact, in my personal experience, brain fog tends to go away. Many gluten-free friends and readers have felt the same.

» **Can I still enjoy the foods I love?** You sure can, and this book is a great place to start. In this book I've compiled a collection of easy-to-make foods that are commonly asked for, such as chicken nuggets, pizza, corn dogs, and even sugar cookies.

» **Where can I shop for gluten-free products?** You can shop anywhere and everywhere you shop for regular foods. Most chain grocery stores, specialty and health food grocers, and online retailers stock gluten-free products. Some of my favorite gluten-free brands include Ancient Harvest, Bob's Red Mill, and King Arthur Flour.

» **Is gluten-free cooking more expensive?** It may be a bit more expensive at first when you're stocking up on the gluten-free essentials you'll need to kick-start your gluten-free journey, but after that initial investment, eating gluten-free shouldn't be any more expensive than cooking food that contains gluten.

» **Will I still feel satiated after eating a gluten-free meal?** Yes, you sure will. You'll feel satisfied and satiated. Again, gluten-free foods remove the gluten, not the nutrients and substance.

» **Do I really need to worry about cross-contamination?** Yes, you do. Most manufacturers will list information on their websites (or you can call or email) about the possibility of products being cross-contaminated with other possible allergens. If you're worried about cross-contamination, look for food products that are certified gluten-free, as these are far more likely to not be contaminated. Always check packaging for gluten-free labeling to ensure that foods, especially oats, were processed in a completely gluten-free facility.

» **Does eating gluten-free get easier?** Yes, it sure does. In time, reading ingredient lists, as well as cooking and baking, get much easier. You just need to allow yourself some time to adjust to a new normal.

» **Will I lose weight on a gluten-free diet?** I've heard that some people do lose weight, and I've heard the opposite from others. I'd recommend talking with your doctor about whether or not a gluten-free diet is right for you and your current weight status.

Shopping Gluten-Free

Shopping for gluten-free items can be a bit tricky when you are just starting out. Here are my best tips for when you're ready to stock up your gluten-free kitchen:

Shop the perimeter: Most of the time, the outer aisles of the grocery store have the fresh produce and meats—the naturally gluten-free products that should be on your shopping list.

Use an app: You can download apps onto your smartphone that allow you to scan barcodes to see nutrition information, including whether or not a product is gluten-free.

Look for labels: Many stores nowadays have labels for products that are gluten-free. Usually the label has wheat grains with a cross going through it or "Gluten-Free" inside a colored circle. Be on the lookout for those.

Do your homework: Know what you are looking for before you leave your house. This may entail an online search for what an item on your list may look like. This will help you identify the products you need once you are in the store.

Buyer beware: Make sure to double-check the use-by dates on your gluten-free food products. Many gluten-free products lack or have fewer preservatives in them, so they will have to be eaten up sooner than you may be used to.

Essential Alternatives

Here you'll find a list of common food items that contain gluten, along with suggestions on gluten-free items you can replace them with:

» **Instead of flour tortillas ▶ Try corn tortillas:** When you're craving Taco Tuesday, simply choose corn tortillas instead of flour tortillas. Lettuce leaves are also a good option.

» **Instead of soy sauce** ▸ **Try liquid aminos:** Liquid aminos are a soy-based alternative to soy sauce (which tends to contain gluten), with a similar flavor and consistency.

» **Instead of roux** ▸ **Try a cornstarch and water slurry:** When making a roux, skip the wheat flour and use cornstarch instead to thicken sauces. All you need is a bit of cornstarch (or arrowroot starch) mixed in a small bowl with a dash of cool water. Add that to hot sauce and watch it thicken up before your eyes.

» **Instead of traditional pasta** ▸ **Try zoodles, spaghetti squash, or gluten-free pasta:** Zoodles (aka zucchini noodles) and spaghetti squash are two pasta alternatives made from vegetables. They are even in the shape of spaghetti noodles, so you can keep that spaghetti fork twirl dream alive. Store-bought gluten-free pastas have also come a long way in the past few years. Pick up a box and give it a try.

» **Instead of all-purpose flour** ▸ **Try white or brown rice, coconut flour, or all-purpose gluten-free flour blends:** There are so many different types of flour and flour blends available today. Rice flours, coconut flour, almond flour, and cassava flour are growing in popularity because of their wide array of uses. There are also some very high-quality gluten-free flour blends out there that produce the same final baked goods as traditional all-purpose flours.

» **Instead of flour tortilla chips** ▸ **Try corn chips, veggie chips, or bell pepper slices:** That's right—there are many other options other than that boring flour tortilla chip. Use a corn or veggie chip instead, or slice bell peppers into large scoopable pieces and dive right into your favorite gluten-free dip.

» **Instead of crackers** ▸ **Try dehydrated veggie slices or rice cakes:** Dehydrated vegetable chips and rice cakes still give the support and crisp crunch of a cracker as well as the finger food–size portion that is perfect for dipping into sauces or for topping with meat or cheese, or even becoming a bruschetta.

» **Instead of croutons** ▸ **Try nuts:** This trick still gives you that crunch to your salad that you were missing from croutons. Not a nut fan? Sprinkle some seeds, corn tortilla chip pieces, or a pinch of gluten-free bread crumbs on your salad instead.

» **Instead of sandwich wraps** ▶ **Try lettuce wraps:** Lettuce wraps give you the same look and feel of devouring a rolled-up sandwich but without the gluten-containing wrap. Plus, the lettuce wrap gives you an added crunch in each bite. So good.

» **Instead of couscous** ▶ **Try cauliflower:** Yes, you heard me right. Instead of couscous, pulse cauliflower in a food processor and let it slice and dice. Ta-da! Instant "couscous."

Tips for Eating Out

Eating out at restaurants can be a big challenge for people who are going gluten-free. But a few tips can make eating out a bit easier for those of us who need a gluten-free experience.

Grab the gluten-free menu. Many restaurants have gluten-free menus available to patrons; all you need to do is ask for one.

Ask your server. If the restaurant doesn't have a gluten-free menu or you are unsure about the menu, ask your server for clarification. They may know, or they may need to ask the manager or chef to fully answer your questions.

Get the app. There are apps you can download to help you decipher what has gluten and what doesn't. Some apps provide information about food products in stores, and others focus on eating out.

Customize a "safe" dish. When in doubt, tell the server you're gluten-free and request the establishment to create a "safe" dish, such as roasted or grilled chicken breast and steamed veggies. Select gluten-free seasonings or herbs.

Bring your own dips/sauces/extras. When I need to request a safe dish at a restaurant, I typically bring my own seasonings, dressings, or sauce, explaining to the management (if needed) that it is due to dietary need. I've never had a restaurant turn up their nose at this. In fact, they're usually quite happy, and it takes stress off their team.

CHAPTER 2

Creating a Gluten-Free Kitchen

When you first start cooking gluten-free, it can be a bit overwhelming to figure out where to even begin. I started by taking a thorough look at what was already in my kitchen. Most home kitchens store foods for the entire family, whether your family members can tolerate gluten or not. But if you are trying or need to stay gluten-free, this can cause a complicated, confusing problem about which products can be used or eaten. Not to worry, though; there are processes you can set in place to make your new world of gluten-free less stressful. Let's take a deep dive into how your gluten-free kitchen can run.

Gluten Purge

The first step to going gluten-free begins with a deep cleanse of your kitchen counters, food pantry, and refrigerator to remove all the items that have gluten in them. Don't forget about common gluten "traps" (food items you think don't contain gluten but do) that might be lurking in your kitchen.

Double-check the nutrition information, because that box of cornflakes you think is strictly made with corn likely has gluten in it or has been cross-contaminated during the manufacturing process. Other gluten food traps include the following:

» **Barbecue sauces**

» **Premade meal kits**

» **Salad dressings**

» **Spice blends**

» **Sports drinks**

» **Vegetable and sauce mixes**

» **Wing sauces**

You will need to donate or give away traditional pasta noodles, cereal, baking mixes, and even certain that contain gluten. If you can't get rid of these items, label them very clearly so you don't accidentally grab them when you mean to grab gluten-free options. If you have space, you could keep all the gluten-containing items separate from the gluten-free foods.

Go-To Ingredients

I have a set of go-to ingredients that you'll need to make the recipes in this book and anything else your gluten-free desires want to go. Here is my list of essentials.

Arrowroot starch: This starch is like cornstarch, working as a great thickener for gravies, pie fillings, and soups. If you're substituting arrowroot starch for cornstarch, you will likely need a larger amount of arrowroot starch to get the same effect, typically using 1½ times the amount of cornstarch.

Snacking Gluten-Free

Following your gluten purge, you'll want to replace your old favorite snacks with equally delicious gluten-free alternatives. Here are some options.

» One of my favorite gluten-free snack alternatives is substituting bell pepper slices and dip for chips and dip. The bell peppers still give you that sturdy surface to scoop into your favorite gluten-free dips and that crisp crunch that a fried chip provides in every bite.

» Another of my favorite gluten-free snacks is popcorn. Many popcorn options are gluten-free and can give you that salty, buttery snack flavor without the gluten.

» When I need a sweet fix, I'll pop a handful of chocolate chips in my mouth. If sweets are also your thing, then let me recommend choco-late. Dark chocolate, milk chocolate, semisweet baking chocolate … many chocolates (even the bags of baking chips) are gluten-free.

Coconut aminos: I use this ingredient all the time to replace soy sauce (1:1 ratio), a condiment with sneaky gluten. Coconut aminos are derived from coconut and have a very similar taste to soy sauce with a hint of soft sweetness from the coconut.

Cornmeal: Used regularly in gluten-free baking and cooking, cornmeal is not just the key player in corn bread. It adds a nice, savory crisp to the coatings of fried foods and is also sometimes used in baking sweets.

Cornstarch: Cornstarch is used in many gluten-free recipes that need something thickened, for instance, gravies and casseroles. Usually a little bit of cornstarch goes a long way. and many times it needs to be combined with a splash of water, creating a slurry, before it can be added to liquids to thicken them.

Xanthan gum: Xanthan gum is added as a dry ingredient to many gluten-free baked goods. This tasteless ingredient is important in gluten-free baking because it adds the sticky effect in gluten-free doughs.

Power of Gluten-Free Flour

Countless times, friends have complained that gluten-free baked goods are just not good. They are dry, tasteless, and crumbly. I say this does not need to be the case. I have found that I can make the same moist, delicious coffee cake (page 40) that everyone else is enjoying, just the gluten-free way, and have an even better final product. The secret is in the flour combinations you use and how you measure those flours (more on measuring on page 14).

Let me tell you a little bit about my favorite gluten-free flours that I keep stocked in my kitchen and a little bit about why each one is so darn good to cook with.

White rice and brown rice flours: These inexpensive flours are used regularly in gluten-free cooking. The difference between the flours is that the brown rice flour is milled with the husk still intact, whereas the white rice flour has it removed before milling. I use rice flours when baking cookies, cakes, muffins, and savory dough such as pizza crusts. I like Bob's Red Mill brand rice flours because of their quality and affordability and because they are quite easy for many home cooks to find at larger grocery stores.

Coconut flour: This flour is used regularly in gluten-free baking and is particularly good in cakes, cookies, and muffins. It is quite absorbent, so don't be surprised when a recipe asks you to give this flour a few minutes to react with the liquids you have added; it'll suck up the moisture that you add to it. It is a bit trickier to work with than others, so don't just use another flour instead of this one. Use it only when specified in recipes.

Tapioca flour: This flour can be used as a thickener in recipes. It is also great at adding that chewy texture to gluten-free baked goods that may otherwise be missing that soft, moist bounce.

Milk powder: Also known as powdered milk, this white powder is considered a nonperishable because it's milk in dried form. Using milk powder as a dry ingredient will add a touch of creaminess and sweetness to baked goods. It will also help add that insanely delicious golden brown crust to baked goodies. Again, I highly recommend Bob's Red Mill brand for the quality, accessibility, and affordability.

HOMEMADE GLUTEN-FREE BAKING MIX

Some recipes in this book call for gluten-free Bisquick mix, which can be found in stores, but if you don't have access to it, you can make it from scratch in under a minute. This recipe will give you enough to make a few decadent cakes. Simply combine all the ingredients and use in a 1:1 ratio.

2 cups white rice flour

1¼ cups coconut flour

1 cup milk powder

½ cup granulated sugar

½ cup cornstarch

1 tablespoon baking powder

1 teaspoon baking soda

½ teaspoon salt

Tools and Equipment

I am pretty basic when it comes to kitchen tools in my own home. I don't want to create meals that need specialized equipment because more tools mean more clutter and more cleaning. That said, there are a few pieces of equipment that you will find very helpful when creating recipes from this book, and they're tools that you likely already have.

Kitchen scale: A kitchen scale is very helpful when you need to measure ingredients by weight. This one isn't a necessity, but it is definitely a nice luxury to have.

Mixing bowls: My set of small, medium, and large mixing bowls comes in handy on a daily basis. You will be using them for the recipes in this book.

Stand mixer: When it comes to baking and creating a perfectly smooth dough, I always trust my stand mixer. If you have a hand mixer, that will work, too, although you may have to put a little more effort into creating the same effect.

Wire strainer spoon: This inexpensive tool has become priceless to me, helping me easily and safely remove deep-fried goodies from boiling hot oil.

Wok or skillet: When frying or sautéing up a quick vegetable dish, I love using my wok, but a nonstick skillet will do fine; it'll just use more oil to get the job done.

Measuring Gluten-Free Flour

Measuring out gluten-free flour is a little bit different than measuring wheat flour, which measures out the same regardless of brand. Measuring gluten-free flour is a bit more complex because different brands use different ingredients and/or sizes of grains. The coarseness of the flour grains in the blend will affect how it packs into measuring cups. Therefore, I strongly encourage you to measure by weight, using a kitchen scale for more consistent results. Kitchen scales can be used to weigh both dry and wet ingredients. Make sure that the scale is on a flat surface and calibrate it regularly for the best results.

If you don't have a kitchen scale, don't worry. You can still create amazing dishes by measuring by volume using measuring cups. Just make sure that you use a liquid measuring cup for liquids and dry measuring cups for dry ingredients.

When using dry measuring cups, use a spoon to fill it with the dry ingredient until the ingredient reaches the top of the measuring cup. If it is a little heaped, use the flat edge of a knife to level it off. Never use the measuring cup to scoop the ingredient from its bag or pour the ingredient directly into the measuring cup. These techniques will pack the measuring cup too tightly with the dry ingredient, leaving you with too much of that product, which increases the chance of producing a dry or crumbly final dish. *Always* spoon dry ingredients into their respective measuring cups.

About the Recipes

To ease you into gluten-free cooking, I've made it a point to only include recipes that are unintimidating and easy to follow. I also include tips for the recipes, such as ingredient swaps, prep tips, helpful hacks, and extra information about the recipe.

The book is broken down into chapters according to meal. Chapter 3 (page 19) is my collection of lovely breakfast and brunch recipes to start the day off right.

This is followed by my favorite beginner-friendly snacks and appetizers in chapter 4 (page 43). Chapter 5 is all about the best soups, salads, and sides (page 63) before getting your main course taken care of. You will find my collection of main course dishes in chapters 6 (page 81) and 7 (page 103), meatless mains and meat and seafood, respectively. No meal is complete without dessert, so I've included my favorite beginner-ready desserts in chapter 8 (page 135), so you don't leave your family table without a sweet fix. And because I did not want to leave anything out, I've also compiled a final chapter with all the little details. Chapter 9 (page 151) brings it all home with dips, dressings, and sauces, because no salad is complete without dressing, no chip complete without its dip, and no meat complete without its sauce.

To make these recipes even easier for you to navigate, I've also included recipe labels for each recipe. Here are the labels to watch for.

» **One pot:** I love this category of recipe because I loathe doing the dishes. One-pot (or dish, bowl, etc.) recipes use just one pot to create the final product.

» **5 ingredient:** There are only five ingredients or fewer in a recipe with this label. These recipes are great when you haven't had a chance to go to the store to buy groceries in a while. You don't need many ingredients to make a delicious dish.

» **30 minutes or less:** Perfect for busy weeknights or those days when you're running short on time, these recipes take 30 minutes or less, start to finish, and many of them are even 15 minutes or less.

» **Dairy-free:** As the name suggests, these recipes either contain no milk products, including butter and cheese.

» **Nut-free:** These recipes contain no tree nuts or coconut.

» **Low-carb:** If you are counting carbs, pay close attention to the collection of low-carb recipes in the book.

» **Vegan:** I know some readers are not only starting out on their gluten-free journey but may also be considering going vegan. As such, there are plenty of vegan options to choose from.

» **Vegetarian:** Anyone looking to make meatless recipes should find the recipes under this category delightful. Most of my recipes can be made without the addition of meat, and those that are meatless to begin with are labeled in this category.

7-Day Meal Plan

Meal planning makes getting meals on the dinner table a little easier. You can choose recipes that fit your wants, needs, and schedule. It also allows you to use up ingredients you already have and spend less at the grocery store when you pair like-ingredient dishes together and cook them in close succession to one another.

To get you started on your gluten-free journey, here is a quick and easy seven-day meal plan for you to dabble with. Feel free to adjust it as needed.

Day 1

Breakfast: Sausage and Egg Quinoa Bowls (page 38)

Lunch: Sesame-Ginger Chicken Chopped Salad (page 67)

Snack: Quick al Fresco Bruschetta (page 53)

Dinner: Caprese Casserole Bake (page 88)

Day 2

Breakfast: Spinach, Bacon, and Mushroom Quiche (page 26)

Lunch: Chicken Salad (page 118)

Snack: Parmesan Crisp Dippers (page 49)

Dinner: Stuffed Mushrooms (page 98)

Day 3

Breakfast: Iced Lemon Loaf (page 36)

Lunch: Garlic-Herbed Orzo and Vegetables (page 92)

Snack: Zucchini Bites (page 55)

Dinner: Roasted Honey-Garlic Pork and Vegetables (page 121)

Day 4

Breakfast: Easy Breakfast Tacos (page 30)

Lunch: Garlic-Avocado Pasta (page 85)

Snack: Pepperoni Pizza Bites (page 60)

Dinner: Fresh Fish Piccata (page 104)

Day 5

Breakfast: Tex-Mex Egg Bites (page 37)

Lunch: Thai-Inspired Turkey Lettuce Wraps (page 122)

Snack: Jalapeño Poppers (page 48)

Dinner: Blackened Fish Fillets (page 119)

Day 6

Breakfast: Biscuits and Gravy Breakfast Casserole (page 32)

Lunch: Sweet Poppy Seed Salad (page 73)

Snack: Crispy Fish Sticks (page 46)

Dinner: Pork Chops with Creamy Gravy (page 108)

Day 7

Breakfast: Glazed Donut Holes (page 20)

Lunch: Grilled Caesar Salad (page 70)

Snack: Cheesy Flatbread (page 56)

Dinner: Fish and Chips (page 124)

Glazed Donut Holes, page 20

Breakfast and Brunch

Glazed Donut Holes

Prep time: 10 minutes, plus 1 hour 20 minutes to rise **Cook time:** 10 minutes

Close your eyes for a second and imagine fluffy balls of sweet dough quickly fried to a golden crisp on their edges. Then these dreamy donut holes are dipped into a sweet sugar glaze that's given a pinch of time to harden, making these the most amazing, poppable donut holes. Now open your eyes and get to baking! **Makes 36 donut holes**

1¼ to 1½ cups heavy
  cream, divided
½ (¾-ounce) packet instant
  quick-rise yeast
1 cup white rice flour
½ cup brown rice flour
½ cup potato starch
¼ cup tapioca flour
2 teaspoons xanthan gum
1 large egg
4 tablespoons (½ stick)
  unsalted butter, melted
  and cooled to room
  temperature
2 tablespoons
  granulated sugar
½ teaspoon salt
Oil, for frying
2½ cups powdered sugar

1. In a small bowl, warm ¾ cup of cream on high power for 20 to 30 seconds, or until warm. Slowly stir in the yeast and allow the mixture to rest for about 5 minutes, or until it starts to form bubbles.

2. In a medium bowl, combine the white rice flour, brown rice flour, potato starch, tapioca flour, and xanthan gum, and stir until well combined. Set aside 2 tablespoons of this flour mix.

3. In the bowl of a stand mixer, combine the cream and yeast mixture, egg, butter, granulated sugar, and salt. Using the dough hook attachment, mix the ingredients together using the lowest setting. Slowly add the flour mixture, about 1 cup at a time. A thick, smooth dough should form. If it is still not thick, add the reserved 2 tablespoons of flour mixture and remix using a slow speed setting.

4. Detach the bowl from the mixer, cover it with a clean kitchen towel, and let the dough rise for 1 hour in a warm place.

5. Place a large piece of parchment paper on the counter and drop the dough down on it. Roll the dough between your hands into gumball-size balls. Allow the dough balls to rest on the parchment paper for 15 to 20 minutes, with the same kitchen towel that covered the bowl also covering the balls.

6. While the dough balls are resting, pour cooking oil into a saucepan or wok over medium heat to a depth of at least 3 inches. Line a plate with paper towels.

7. Working in small batches, carefully dunk the balls into the hot oil to fry. Cook for 30 to 90 seconds, or until the balls turn a light golden brown on all sides. Use a wire strainer spoon to flip the dough balls for even cooking on all sides. Transfer to the prepared plate to cool.

8. Make the glaze by combining the powdered sugar and remaining ½ to ¾ cup of cream in a medium bowl and stirring well until smooth. Dip each donut hole in the glaze to coat and set it on a wire cooling rack to harden.

Per serving (2 donut holes): Calories: 244; Total Fat: 12g; Saturated Fat: 6g; Cholesterol: 44mg; Carbohydrates: 32g; Fiber: 1g; Sodium: 99mg; Protein: 2g

Mini Raspberry Muffins

Prep time: 15 minutes **Cook time:** 20 minutes

This mini muffin recipe is a great way to have a delicious breakfast on the go. I make these raspberry-filled bite-size muffins to have ready for breakfast throughout my busy workweek. They do a great job of keeping me satiated until my lunch break. If you are looking for a dairy-free muffin, substitute the butter with an equal amount of almond butter. **Makes 18 muffins**

Gluten-free cooking spray, for coating the muffin tin (optional)

½ cup coconut flour

2 tablespoons sugar

1 teaspoon baking powder

½ teaspoon baking soda

¼ teaspoon salt

2 large eggs, at room temperature, beaten

½ cup vanilla almond milk, close to room temperature

½ cup honey

⅓ cup coconut oil, melted

1 tablespoon apple cider vinegar

1 tablespoon unsalted butter, at room temperature

1 teaspoon vanilla extract

⅔ cup fresh raspberries

1. Preheat the oven to 350°F. Line a mini muffin tin with muffin liners or spray it with cooking spray.

2. In a medium bowl, combine the flour, sugar, baking powder, baking soda, and salt.

3. In a large bowl, combine the eggs, almond milk, honey, oil, vinegar, butter, and vanilla.

4. Slowly add the dry ingredients to the wet ingredients. Using a mixer, mix until well combined. Allow the dough to set and thicken for 5 minutes.

5. Fold in the raspberries and fill each mini muffin cup three-fourths full of batter.

6. Cook for 13 to 18 minutes, or until the edges are golden brown and a toothpick inserted into the center of a muffin comes out clean.

7. Remove from the oven and allow to cool slightly before transferring the muffins to a cooling rack. Cool completely before serving. Store leftovers at room temperature in an airtight container or a plastic storage bag for up to 3 days.

Prep Tip: You can use this recipe for regular-size muffins. Bake them for 3 to 5 extra minutes and wait a few extra minutes (3 to 4 minutes) before popping them out of the muffin tin to allow them to set up properly.

Per serving (1 muffin): Calories: 148; Total Fat: 7g; Saturated Fat: 5g; Cholesterol: 22mg; Carbohydrates: 19g; Fiber: 5g; Sodium: 95mg; Protein: 4g

Spiced Banana Bread Bars

Prep time: 10 minutes **Cook time:** 25 minutes

One of the easiest ways to use up ripe or overripe bananas is to put them into soft, moist, spiced banana bread bars. This recipe gives bananas a second chance at deliciousness with tender pieces of gently spiced bread with hints of banana in every bite. **Serves 12**

Gluten-free cooking spray, for coating the loaf pan
1 cup sugar
⅔ cup brown rice flour
⅔ cup tapioca flour
⅓ cup coconut flour
1 teaspoon baking soda
½ teaspoon ground cinnamon
½ teaspoon ground cloves
½ teaspoon ground nutmeg
½ teaspoon salt
¼ teaspoon baking powder
2 large eggs, beaten
⅓ cup water
⅓ cup unsalted butter, melted
2 to 3 very ripe medium bananas, peeled and mashed

1. Preheat the oven to 350°F. Spray the cups of a mini loaf pan with cooking spray. Set the pan on a baking sheet.

2. In a large bowl, combine the sugar, rice flour, tapioca flour, coconut flour, baking soda, cinnamon, cloves, nutmeg, salt, and baking powder. Mix well.

3. Stir in the eggs, water, and butter, then add the bananas. Allow to rest for 5 minutes.

4. Spoon the batter into the bottom two-thirds of each mini loaf cup. Bake for 18 to 23 minutes, or until the edges are nicely golden brown.

5. Remove from the oven and allow to cool and set for 5 to 10 minutes in the loaf pan before moving the mini bread bars to a cooling rack.

6. Store leftover bars in an airtight container or plastic storage bag at room temperature for up to 4 days.

Per serving: Calories: 209; Total Fat: 6g; Saturated Fat: 4g; Cholesterol: 44mg; Carbohydrates: 36g; Fiber: 2g; Sodium: 255mg; Protein: 3g

Sweet Grits and Berries

Prep time: 5 minutes **Cook time:** 10 minutes

Grits are a longtime traditional Southern breakfast staple and are just as popular today as they were decades ago. They're served savory, usually with cheese and herbs, or sweet, as in this recipe. Either way you choose to eat grits is a choice well made. **Serves 4 to 6**

1 to 2 cups fresh
  berries, sliced
1 to 3 tablespoons
  granulated sugar
4 cups milk of choice
½ teaspoon salt
2 tablespoons packed light
  brown sugar
3 tablespoons honey, plus
  more for drizzling
1 tablespoon unsalted butter
1 cup quick grits (not instant)

1. In a medium bowl, mix the berries and the granulated sugar together.

2. In a large saucepan, bring the milk, salt, brown sugar, honey, and butter to a simmer over medium heat. Once simmering, mix the grits in slowly while continuously stirring.

3. Reduce the heat to low, cover, and allow the grits to simmer for 3 to 4 minutes, then uncover and continuously stir them for 2 to 3 more minutes. Remove from the heat.

4. Pour the grits into serving bowls, add the sugared berries on top and an extra drizzle of honey, and enjoy. Store leftovers in an airtight container in the refrigerator for up to 2 days.

Helpful Hack: If you like thicker grits, reduce the amount of milk by ¼ cup, and if you like them a bit thinner, add another ¼ cup of milk.

Per serving: Calories: 356; Total Fat: 11g; Saturated Fat: 6g; Cholesterol: 32mg; Carbohydrates: 55g; Fiber: 2g; Sodium: 667mg; Protein: 10g

Spinach, Bacon, and Mushroom Quiche

Prep time: 10 minutes **Cook time:** 45 minutes

If you're in the mood for breakfast for dinner, this quiche is the way to go. To make this recipe dairy-free, use olive oil instead of butter and dairy-free shredded cheese instead of Gruyère. To make it vegetarian, omit the bacon and replace it with ½ cup of your favorite chopped vegetables. **Serves 8**

2 tablespoons
  unsalted butter
½ cup diced sweet onion
1 cup fresh spinach
½ cup chopped mushrooms
1 (9-inch) frozen gluten-free
  pie crust
5 or 6 slices cooked bacon,
  cut into bits
1½ cups shredded
  Gruyère cheese
4 large eggs, beaten
1 cup milk of choice
½ teaspoon garlic powder
Salt
Freshly ground black pepper
Fresh thyme leaves,
  for garnish

1. Preheat the oven to 375°F.

2. In a medium skillet, heat the butter over medium heat until melted and add the onion, spinach, and mushrooms. Cook, stirring occasionally, for 3 to 4 minutes, or until the onion is soft, translucent, and fragrant. Remove from the heat.

3. While the onion mixture is cooking, set the pie crust on a large rimmed baking sheet.

4. In a large bowl, combine the bacon, cheese, eggs, milk, and garlic powder. Season with salt and pepper. Stir. Add the cooked onion mixture to the bowl and stir to mix thoroughly.

5. Pour the mixture into the pie crust. Bake on the baking sheet for 33 to 37 minutes, until the top is golden brown and the center is just barely jiggly when moved.

6. Allow to cool for 5 minutes before cutting into slices. Sprinkle the top of each slice with thyme and serve. Store leftover quiche in an airtight container in the refrigerator for up to 3 days.

Ingredient Swap: This quiche is fantastic with any favorite chopped vegetables you have on hand. Feel free to swap out either the mushrooms or spinach for equal amounts of another veggie. Just make sure that they are of equal amounts, or you may have too much filling for the pie crust.

Per serving: Calories: 291; Total Fat: 21g; Saturated Fat: 9g; Cholesterol: 134mg; Carbohydrates: 11g; Fiber: 1g; Sodium: 487mg; Protein: 14g

Cowboy Frittata

Prep time: 20 minutes **Cook time:** 35 minutes

This spin on a popular breakfast choice, the Western omelet, still brings you all the flavors of the Wild West but in a more refined package, the frittata. This recipe allows you to make swaps and substitutions at will, so every cowboy and cowgirl gets their slice of breakfast heaven. **Serves 8**

3 tablespoons cooking oil

1 large Russet potato, cut into 1-inch cubes

1 cup chopped bell pepper

2 cups cooked ground gluten-free sausage

½ cup diced onion

½ teaspoon minced garlic

1 teaspoon dried thyme or 1 tablespoon chopped fresh thyme

1 teaspoon garlic powder

6 to 8 fresh sage leaves, chopped

½ teaspoon paprika

Salt

Freshly ground black pepper

8 large eggs, beaten with 2 tablespoons water

1. Preheat the oven to 375°F. Heat an oven-safe skillet over medium heat with the oil coating the bottom and sides of the skillet. Add the potato and cook for about 10 minutes, or until fork tender.

2. Add the bell pepper, sausage, onion, garlic, thyme, garlic powder, sage, and paprika. Season with salt and pepper and sauté for about 5 minutes, or until the bell pepper has softened.

3. Reduce the heat to low and add the egg and water mixture, stirring once to mix thoroughly, then leave it undisturbed. Cook for 4 to 5 minutes, or until the egg just starts to set or firm slightly.

4. Transfer to the oven and bake for 10 to 12 minutes, or until the edges are golden brown and are starting to separate from the skillet.

5. Remove from the oven and allow to cool for a few minutes before slicing and serving.

6. Store leftovers in an airtight container in the refrigerator for up to 3 days. Reheat a slice of frittata on a microwave-safe plate on high for 45 to 90 seconds.

Helpful Hack: Because the skillet will be coming out of a hot oven, its handle will be scorching hot. To remind yourself of the hot handle, put an oven mitt on top of the handle once it is out of the oven. This way, even if you do accidentally grab the handle, you won't get burned.

Per serving: Calories: 359; Total Fat: 26g; Saturated Fat: 7g; Cholesterol: 218mg; Carbohydrates: 13g; Fiber: 1g; Sodium: 778mg; Protein: 18g

Easy Breakfast Tacos

Prep time: 5 minutes **Cook time:** 15 minutes

Who wouldn't want to be holding toasted tortillas filled with warm meat and fluffy eggs, all seasoned with a simple taco seasoning and topped with fresh salsa and shredded cheese? You can have breakfast tacos in your hands in minutes with this easy recipe. **Serves 4 to 6**

1 tablespoon cooking oil

2 cups chopped or crumbled cooked protein of choice (see tip)

½ teaspoon garlic powder

½ teaspoon paprika

¼ teaspoon dried oregano

¼ teaspoon ground cumin

¼ teaspoon salt

8 large eggs, beaten

2 tablespoons milk

1 bag gluten-free corn tortillas

1 to 2 cups pico de gallo

Salsa, for garnish

Shredded cheese, for garnish

Fresh chopped cilantro, for garnish

1. In a large nonstick skillet, heat the oil over medium heat for 1 to 2 minutes. Add the protein, garlic powder, paprika, oregano, cumin, and salt and stir until evenly coated and the meat is heated through.

2. Move the meat to the outer edges of the skillet. Add the eggs and milk to the center and allow them to scramble, stirring occasionally, leaving the meat toward the outside of the skillet and the eggs toward the center.

3. While the eggs are scrambling, in a small skillet, warm the tortillas over low heat. Once the edges of each tortilla start to bubble up a bit, flip the tortilla and heat for an additional 30 seconds before transferring to a plate. Keep them covered with a towel until ready to eat.

4. Once the eggs are completely scrambled, fold in the pico de gallo and stir until everything is evenly combined. Remove from the heat. Place the egg and meat mixture into each warmed tortilla and top with salsa, cheese, and cilantro, then serve.

5. Once cooled, store the leftover tacos in an airtight container in the refrigerator for up to 3 days. To reheat them, cover them on a microwave-safe plate and microwave on high for 60 to 90 seconds, or until hot.

Ingredient Swap: I like to use up any leftover meat from the previous day in this recipe. Chicken, steak pieces, turkey, ground beef, pork slices, etc. are all good. If you are vegetarian, trying substituting any leftover beans for the meat in this recipe.

Per serving: Calories: 434; Total Fat: 21g; Saturated Fat: 5g; Cholesterol: 425mg; Carbohydrates: 28g; Fiber: 1g; Sodium: 793mg; Protein: 33g

NUT-FREE

Biscuits and Gravy Breakfast Casserole

Prep time: 20 minutes **Cook time:** 50 minutes

Growing up in the South, I learned that everything is better with gravy. This holds true with this breakfast casserole; it is perfectly smothered in a thick white gravy. Even though this is a breakfast casserole, in the South we will eat this for any meal. **Serves 8**

FOR THE BISCUITS

Gluten-free cooking spray,
    for coating the baking dish
¾ cup gluten-free Bisquick
    mix or Homemade
    Gluten-Free Baking Mix
    (page 13)
⅓ cup milk of choice
2 tablespoons unsalted
    butter, melted
1 large egg, beaten

FOR THE CASSEROLE

1½ to 2 cups precooked
    breakfast sausage
    crumbles
6 large eggs, beaten
½ cup milk of choice
1 cup shredded
    cheese, divided
¼ to ½ cup chopped
    cooked bacon

TO MAKE THE BISCUITS

1. Preheat the oven to 375°F. Spray a 9-by-13-inch glass baking dish with cooking spray. In a medium bowl, combine the baking mix, milk, butter, and egg and place the dough in the bottom of the prepared baking dish.

TO MAKE THE CASSEROLE

2. Spread the sausage in a single even layer on top of the biscuit dough. In a medium bowl, combine the eggs, milk, and ½ cup of cheese and mix thoroughly, then pour it over the dough and sausage.

3. Bake for 35 to 40 minutes, or until the edges of the casserole are a nice golden brown and any liquid around the edges of the dish is bubbling. Remove from the oven, sprinkle with the remaining ½ cup of cheese and the bacon, and allow it to set for 5 minutes.

FOR THE GRAVY

2 tablespoons unsalted butter

¼ cup gluten-free flour blend

1¾ cups chicken broth

½ cup heavy cream

¼ to ½ teaspoon salt

½ teaspoon freshly ground
black pepper

TO MAKE THE GRAVY

4. Meanwhile, in a medium saucepan, melt the butter over medium heat. Add the flour blend and continuously mix for 30 seconds, or until the liquids are fully absorbed. Add the chicken broth, ⅓ cup at a time, waiting until the gravy returns to a simmer before stirring and adding the next ⅓ cup. Do the same with the cream. Add the salt and pepper and simmer for 5 to 10 minutes. Remove from the heat and pour over the casserole, then serve. Store room-temperature leftovers in an airtight container in the refrigerator for up to 3 days.

Ingredient Swap: To make this dish dairy-free, simply substitute the butter with dairy-free butter, use dairy-free shredded Cheddar cheese, and use unsweetened almond milk for the milk of choice and heavy cream (bearing in mind that this dish will now contain nuts).

Per serving: Calories: 368; Total Fat: 24g; Saturated Fat: 13g; Cholesterol: 221mg; Carbohydrates: 19g; Fiber: 1g; Sodium: 694mg; Protein: 17g

Cinnamon Roll French Toast Casserole

Prep time: 10 minutes **Cook time:** 45 minutes

If French toast could join forces with cinnamon rolls, this would definitely be the irresistible result. Once out of the oven and drizzled with icing, this dish is best scooped out and served warm. It's also great reheated the next day—that is, if you even have leftovers. **Serves 8**

Gluten-free cooking spray, for coating the baking dish
1 loaf gluten-free bread, cut into cubes
7 large eggs, beaten
2 cups milk of choice (I use whole milk), plus 7 tablespoons
¼ cup honey
1½ tablespoons vanilla extract
2½ teaspoons ground cinnamon, divided
½ teaspoon ground nutmeg (optional)
5 tablespoons cold unsalted, sliced
½ cup packed light brown sugar
3 cups powdered sugar

1. Preheat the oven to 375°F. Spray a 9-by-13-inch glass baking dish with cooking spray.

2. Spread the bread cubes in the bottom of the baking dish.

3. In a medium bowl, combine the eggs, 2 cups of milk, the honey, vanilla, 1½ teaspoons of cinnamon, and the nutmeg (if using) and stir thoroughly. Pour the egg mixture over the bread, making sure all the bread cubes are coated. Put it in the refrigerator.

4. In a small bowl, stir together the remaining 1 teaspoon of cinnamon, the butter, and the brown sugar until well combined and crumbly. Sprinkle the mixture on top of the chilled casserole and cover with aluminum foil.

5. Bake for 25 minutes, remove the foil, and bake for an additional 20 minutes.

6. While the casserole is baking in a bowl, combine the powdered sugar and remaining 7 tablespoons of milk until a smooth icing forms.

7. Remove the casserole from the oven, drizzle with the icing, and allow to cool and set for 5 to 10 minutes before serving warm.

Ingredient Swap: To make this recipe dairy-free, use almond milk and dairy free butter (bearing in mind that this dish will now contain nuts).

Per serving: Calories: 546; Total Fat: 15g; Saturated Fat: 8g; Cholesterol: 189mg; Carbohydrates: 89g; Fiber: 6g; Sodium: 427mg; Protein: 14g

Iced Lemon Loaf

Prep time: 5 minutes **Cook time:** 55 minutes

This light, fluffy, and moist lemon cake is a refreshingly sweet way to start the day, especially when paired with your favorite morning cup of joe or hot tea. Grab a second piece before these slices are all gone. **Serves 8**

Gluten-free cooking spray, for coating the loaf pan
1½ cups gluten-free baking flour blend
1 cup granulated sugar
2 teaspoons baking powder
½ teaspoon salt
2 large eggs
½ cup milk
8 tablespoons (1 stick) unsalted butter, at room temperature
7 to 8 tablespoons freshly squeezed lemon juice, divided
¾ cup powdered sugar

1. Preheat the oven to 350°F. Spray a glass loaf pan with cooking spray.

2. In a large bowl, combine the flour, granulated sugar, baking powder, and salt and mix well. Add the eggs, milk, butter, and 3 tablespoons of lemon juice and stir until a smooth batter forms.

3. Pour the batter into the prepared loaf pan and bake on the middle rack for 50 to 55 minutes, or until the edges and top of the loaf are golden brown and a toothpick inserted into the center of the loaf is pulled out clean. Remove from the oven. Allow to cool for 10 minutes, then transfer to a wire rack to cool completely.

4. While the loaf is cooling, make the lemon icing by mixing the powdered sugar and remaining 4 to 5 tablespoons of lemon juice in a small bowl and stirring until it's smooth. Pour the icing over the room-temperature loaf and let sit for 30 minutes to 1 hour, or until the icing hardens. Slice and serve.

Per serving: Calories: 332; Total Fat: 13g; Saturated Fat: 8g; Cholesterol: 79mg; Carbohydrates: 52g; Fiber: 1g; Sodium: 263mg; Protein: 3g

Tex-Mex Egg Bites

Prep time: 5 minutes **Cook time:** 30 minutes

This recipe is part egg muffin and part egg soufflé. The combination of garlic, cheese, and pico de gallo gives this breakfast finger food a punch of Tex-Mex flavor. It's a bite-size party for your palate to start the morning off just right. **Serves 4 to 6**

Gluten-free cooking spray, for coating the muffin tin
5 large eggs, beaten
1½ teaspoons milk of choice
2 teaspoons dried minced onion
¼ teaspoon freshly ground black pepper
¼ teaspoon garlic salt
6 teaspoons feta cheese crumbles
6 teaspoons pico de gallo
6 teaspoons bacon bits (optional)
½ teaspoon paprika

1. Preheat the oven to 375°F. Spray a mini muffin tin with cooking spray.

2. In a large bowl, stir together the eggs, milk, onion, pepper, and garlic salt.

3. Divide the cheese, pico de gallo, and bacon (if using) evenly among each muffin cup. Pour in enough of the egg mixture to fill each muffin cup.

4. Sprinkle each cup with a pinch of paprika and bake for 26 to 28 minutes, or until the tops are fluffy and golden brown and the edges are no longer bubbling with liquid. Remove from the oven. Cool for 3 to 4 minutes before removing from the muffin tin.

5. Store leftover egg bites in an airtight storage container in the refrigerator for up to 48 hours.

Ingredient Swap: Easily make these vegetarian by subbing chopped mushrooms or a crumbled plant-based meat alternative for the bacon bits.

Per serving: Calories: 72; Total Fat: 4g; Saturated Fat: 2g; Cholesterol: 158mg; Carbohydrates: 1g; Fiber: 0g; Sodium: 114mg; Protein: 6g

Sausage and Egg Quinoa Bowls

Prep time: 5 minutes **Cook time:** 20 minutes

This warm, wholesome breakfast will have you hooked and coming back for a second helping. It combines the best savory breakfast ingredients and the best seasoned vegetables, all tossed together into bowls for on-the-go mornings and leisurely brunches alike. **Serves 4**

2 cups water

1 cup quinoa, rinsed and drained

Pinch salt

2 tablespoons olive oil

1½ tablespoons minced garlic

¾ cup diced onion

Precooked breakfast sausage links, sliced, or precooked breakfast sausage crumbles

1 cup grape or cherry tomatoes, halved

4 large eggs, beaten

1 bag baby spinach, coarsely chopped

2 ounces goat cheese crumbles

1. In a medium saucepan, bring the water, quinoa, and salt to a boil. Reduce the heat to medium-low, cover, and cook for 10 to 15 minutes, or until the water is absorbed.

2. While the quinoa is cooking, in a large skillet, heat the oil over medium heat. Stir in the garlic and onion and cook for 2 to 3 minutes, or until the onion has softened and become fragrant. Add the sausage and tomatoes and cook for 3 to 4 minutes, or until the tomatoes have started to reduce and wilt.

3. Move the vegetables to one side of the skillet to continue cooking. Add the eggs to the other half of the skillet. Allow the eggs to cook, stirring them occasionally, until they have turned into a fluffy white and yellow scramble. Then add the spinach and stir everything together until the spinach has wilted and reduced dramatically. Remove from the heat.

4. Once the quinoa is done cooking, remove it from the heat and stir in the cheese until thoroughly combined. Place one-fourth of the quinoa in a bowl and top with one-fourth of the skillet scramble; repeat for the other 3 bowls. Enjoy this dish while it is still warm and steamy.

Cooking Tip: Not all of the spinach will fit into the skillet at one time; however, it will reduce nicely once properly cooked. I highly recommend adding the spinach one handful at a time and letting it wilt before adding more.

Per serving: Calories: 431; Total Fat: 22g; Saturated Fat: 6g; Cholesterol: 237mg; Carbohydrates: 36g; Fiber: 6g; Sodium: 416mg; Protein: 22g

Moist Coffee Cake

Prep time: 5 minutes **Cook time:** 1 hour

Coffee cake is designed to be eaten at breakfast and therefore should go beautifully with your favorite cup of coffee. This tall, fluffy cake with the perfect amount of sponginess and moisture fits the bill. Every tender piece of sweet cake is topped with a melted cinnamon-sugar crumble. Enjoy your mornings. **Serves 12**

FOR THE COFFEE CAKE

Gluten-free cooking spray, for coating the baking dish
1½ cups granulated sugar
1 cup white rice flour
½ cup brown rice flour
½ cup potato starch
¼ cup tapioca flour
1 tablespoon baking powder
2 teaspoons xanthan gum
¾ teaspoon salt
3 large eggs, beaten
¾ cup milk
12 tablespoons (1½ sticks) unsalted butter, at room temperature
2 tablespoons almond extract

FOR THE CINNAMON CRUMBLE

1 cup packed light brown sugar
½ cup granulated sugar
8 tablespoons (1 stick) unsalted butter, at room temperature
1 tablespoon ground cinnamon
½ cup brown rice flour

TO MAKE THE COFFEE CAKE

1. Preheat the oven to 350°F. Spray a 2-quart baking dish with cooking spray.

2. In a large bowl, combine the granulated sugar, white rice flour, brown rice flour, potato starch, tapioca flour, baking powder, xanthan gum, and salt and mix well. Add the eggs, milk, butter, and almond extract and stir until well combined and a smooth batter forms.

3. Pour the batter into the bottom of the prepared baking dish. Bake on the middle rack for 20 minutes.

TO MAKE THE CINNAMON CRUMBLE

4. While the cake is cooking, combine the brown sugar, granulated sugar, butter, and cinnamon in a medium bowl. Once combined, add the brown rice flour and stir until just combined.

5. Remove the coffee cake from the oven and sprinkle an even thin layer of the crumble on top of the cake. Return the cake to the oven for another 35 to 40 minutes, or until the edges and top of the loaf are golden brown and a toothpick inserted into the center of the loaf is pulled out clean. Remove from the oven. Allow to cool for 10 minutes before cutting into squares and serving.

Ingredient Swap: To make this recipe nut-free, use vanilla extract instead of almond extract.

Per serving: Calories: 527; Total Fat: 21g; Saturated Fat: 13g; Cholesterol: 99mg; Carbohydrates: 82g; Fiber: 2g; Sodium: 333mg; Protein: 5g

Mini Corn Dogs, page 58

Snacks and Appetizers

Crispy Tortilla Chips

Prep time: 5 minutes **Cook time:** 25 minutes

These chips are a crunchy tropical treat. They give you that crispy perfection you crave without you having to fry them. Carefully watch the chips during the final 5 minutes because they can sometimes burn quickly at the end of the baking session. **Serves 4**

2 tablespoons coconut
  oil, melted
1 tablespoon freshly
  squeezed lime juice
½ teaspoon garlic powder
15 to 20 small gluten-free
  corn tortillas
Coarse sea salt

1. Preheat the oven to 325°F. Line a baking sheet with parchment paper.

2. In a medium bowl, combine the oil, lime juice, and garlic powder and mix well. With a basting brush, lightly apply the oil mixture to both sides of each tortilla.

3. Cut each tortilla into 6 triangles and place on the prepared baking sheet. Sprinkle with salt and cook for 20 to 25 minutes, or until the chips become crispy and lightly browned on the edges and the corners start to curl up. Remove from the oven.

Helpful Hack: Use a rolling pizza slicer to easily cut the tortillas into triangles. You also may need to bake on 2 baking sheets (or bake in batches), depending on the size of the baking sheet and how many chips you have to bake.

Per serving: Calories: 257; Total Fat: 9g; Saturated Fat: 6g; Cholesterol: 0mg; Carbohydrates: 41g; Fiber: 6g; Sodium: 41mg; Protein: 5g

Mozzarella Sticks

Prep time: 5 minutes, plus 30 minutes to freeze **Cook time:** 10 minutes

This recipe turns the mozzarella sticks that everyone loves into something that is gluten-free but still tastes like the original snack. The garlicky gluten-free bread crumb mixture is baked in the oven rather than fried, creating a delicious, less greasy, gluten-free version of an old snacking favorite. **Makes 12 sticks**

2 large eggs, beaten
¾ cup plain gluten-free
   bread crumbs
¾ cup white rice flour
2 tablespoons Italian
   seasoning
1¼ teaspoons garlic powder
½ teaspoon salt
6 mozzarella sticks, halved
   and frozen

1. Preheat the oven to 400°F. Line a baking sheet with parchment paper.

2. Put the eggs in one bowl, the bread crumbs in a separate bowl, and the flour, Italian seasoning, garlic powder, and salt, mixed well, into a third bowl.

3. Take 1 frozen cheese stick half and dip it first into the flour, then into the egg, then back for a second round in the flour, then back into the egg, making sure to coat all sides with each dip. Lastly, dip it into the bread crumbs, pressing the bread crumbs gently into the sides of the stick to make the crumbs stick. Return it to the freezer for 30 minutes. Repeat with the remaining cheese stick halves.

4. Spread the mozzarella sticks out evenly on the prepared baking sheet. Bake for 4 to 6 minutes, or until the cheese is bubbly and browning around the edges. You may want to flip the sticks halfway through the baking process for an evenly cooked golden brown outer crust. Remove from the oven.

Per serving (1 mozzarella stick): Calories: 98; Total Fat: 4g; Saturated Fat: 2g; Cholesterol: 39mg; Carbohydrates: 12g; Fiber: 1g; Sodium: 208mg; Protein: 5g

Crispy Fish Sticks

Prep time: 5 minutes **Cook time:** 20 minutes

These made-from-scratch oven-baked fish sticks are the best that will ever come out of the oven. This quick recipe uses only a handful of ingredients that you likely already have in your kitchen, and it takes only minutes to bake the tender, fresh insides and crisp, golden, savory coating on the outside. As a bonus, there are very few dishes to clean up afterward.

Makes 12 sticks

3 tablespoons gluten-free
 mayonnaise
1 large tilapia fillet, cut
 into strips
½ cup plain gluten-free
 bread crumbs
½ cup grated
 parmesan cheese
1 teaspoon garlic powder
1 teaspoon onion powder
½ teaspoon finely chopped
 fresh parsley
¼ teaspoon paprika
Gluten-free cooking spray,
 for coating the fish sticks

1. Preheat the oven to 400°F. Line a baking sheet with parchment paper.

2. Put the mayonnaise in a medium bowl, drop the fish sticks into the bowl, and coat them evenly.

3. In a zip-top plastic bag, combine the bread crumbs, cheese, garlic powder, onion powder, parsley, and paprika. Add the fish sticks and toss to coat the fish evenly on all sides.

4. Place the breaded fish sticks evenly spaced out on the prepared baking sheet. Lightly spray them with cooking spray.

5. Cook, flipping the sticks halfway through, for 14 to 16 minutes, or until the internal temperature of the fish sticks is 145°F and the desired level of crunch is achieved. Remove from the oven. Allow to cool for 1 to 2 minutes before serving warm.

Per serving (1 fish stick): Calories: 86; Total Fat: 5g; Saturated Fat: 1g; Cholesterol: 19mg; Carbohydrates: 4g; Fiber: 0g; Sodium: 139mg; Protein: 7g

Juicy Meatballs

Prep time: 5 minutes **Cook time:** 15 minutes

These simple yet fantastically juicy and flavorful oven-baked meatballs will turn you into a meatball snob. And they come together without bread crumbs, keeping the carb count low. Roll them up and toss them in the oven for a few minutes, and you have a pile of incredible meatballs for the whole family to devour. **Makes 24 meatballs**

1 pound grass-fed
    ground beef
1 large egg, beaten
1 teaspoon finely
    chopped onion
½ teaspoon minced garlic
1 teaspoon liquid aminos
¼ teaspoon coarse salt
¼ teaspoon freshly ground
    black pepper

1. Preheat the oven to 400°F. Line a plate with paper towels.

2. In a medium bowl, combine the ground beef, egg, onion, garlic, liquid aminos, salt, and pepper and thoroughly mix together with your hands.

3. Roll into 1- to 1½-inch balls (gumball-size) and place 1 in each cup of a mini muffin tin.

4. Bake for 10 minutes, take out of the oven, flip the meatballs, and bake for an additional 5 minutes, or until thoroughly cooked and the outsides are nicely browned. Remove from he oven.

5. Carefully transfer the hot meatballs to the prepared plate to soak up any extra grease.

6. Use immediately or store in the refrigerator in an airtight container. You can also freeze them for later.

Helpful Hack: Looking for an even easier way to get meatballs into perfect balls? Use an ice cream scoop to scoop out the beef mixture.

Per serving (3 meatballs): Calories: 142; Total Fat: 11g; Saturated Fat: 5g; Cholesterol: 61mg; Carbohydrates: 0g; Fiber: 0g; Sodium: 102mg; Protein: 11g

Jalapeño Poppers

Prep time: 5 minutes **Cook time:** 10 minutes

This jalapeño poppers recipe uses crisp bacon crumbles to provide the crunchy topping instead of the typical bread crumbs, but feel free to add gluten-free bread crumbs to the top of the poppers if you'd like. Each bite combines spicy hints with warm, melty cheese and crunch from the tender charred pepper. The perfect snack or appetizer in just 15 minutes. **Serves 8**

4 fresh jalapeños, halved and seeded
1 ounce cream cheese, at room temperature
½ cup shredded cheese (Cheddar or Colby Jack is best)
¼ teaspoon garlic powder
2 bacon slices, cooked and crumbled

1. Preheat the broiler to high. Place the jalapeño halves on a rimmed baking sheet.

2. In a small bowl, combine the cream cheese, shredded cheese, and garlic powder. Stir until well combined.

3. Fill each pepper with equal amounts of the cheese mixture. Broil for 5 to 7 minutes, or until the peppers start to crisp and brown around the edges.

4. Remove from the oven and sprinkle with the bacon crumbles. Allow to cool for 2 to 4 minutes before serving warm.

Serving Tip: I highly recommend drizzling these jalapeño poppers with a bit of honey for a sweet and spicy effect. Sliced scallions (green parts only) are also a huge hit sprinkled on top.

Per serving: Calories: 57; Total Fat: 5g; Saturated Fat: 2g; Cholesterol: 14mg; Carbohydrates: 1g; Fiber: 0g; Sodium: 107mg; Protein: 3g

Parmesan Crisp Dippers

Prep time: 1 minute **Cook time:** 5 minutes

These three-ingredient crispy cheesy dippers are the perfect appetizer or snack for any gluten-free or low-carb eaters and are huge hits at parties. All you need is parmesan, Italian seasoning, garlic powder, and 5 minutes in the oven. **Makes 16 pieces**

1 cup shredded
  parmesan cheese
1 tablespoon garlic powder
1 tablespoon Italian
  seasoning

1. Preheat the oven to 350°F. Line a baking sheet with parchment paper.

2. Place 1-tablespoon heaps of cheese on the baking sheet, spreading each heap out into a thinner circle. Sprinkle each with a pinch of garlic powder and Italian seasoning.

3. Bake for 5 minutes, or until the outer edges become golden brown. Remove from the oven and let sit for 3 to 5 minutes, or until cooled and hardened.

- -

Ingredient Swap: Don't have garlic powder? Try onion powder. Low on Italian seasoning? Swap it out for dried basil. You can swap or adjust the spices in this recipe to your liking.

- -

Per serving: Calories: 28; Total Fat: 2g; Saturated Fat: 1g; Cholesterol: 5mg; Carbohydrates: 1g; Fiber: 0g; Sodium: 113mg; Protein: 2g

Cheesy Potato Skins

Prep time: 15 minutes **Cook time:** 40 minutes

This double cheese appetizer is the perfect finger food for casual get-togethers and will be gone in seconds. Experiment with swapping in different cheeses (e.g., Gouda) and herbs (e.g., rosemary instead of scallions) to mix it up and have fun. Omit the bacon bits for a vegetarian option. **Serves 8**

4 large Russet potatoes
2 teaspoons garlic powder
8 ounces cream cheese, at
    room temperature
2 cups shredded cheese
    (Cheddar or Colby Jack, for
    example)
½ cup bacon bits
2 tablespoons olive oil
Pinch salt
Sliced scallions, green parts
    only, for garnish (optional)

1. Preheat the oven to 400°F.

2. Scrub the potatoes and poke all sides with a fork. Microwave on high power for 5 minutes, flip the potatoes, and microwave for another 5 minutes. Allow to cool for 5 to 10 minutes.

3. While the potatoes are cooling, in a medium bowl, combine the garlic powder, cream cheese, shredded cheese, and bacon bits and stir well.

4. Slice each potato in half lengthwise and scoop out the potato flesh, leaving a slight amount on the inside of each potato skin. Use a basting brush to brush the oil on both sides of each potato skin.

5. Place each potato skin, open-side up, on a baking sheet and sprinkle with the salt. Bake for 8 minutes, flip, sprinkle with salt, and bake for another 8 minutes. Remove from the oven.

6. Place equal amounts of the cheese mixture in each potato skin. Bake for another 12 to 15 minutes, or until the cheese is melted and golden brown on top. Remove from the oven. Allow to cool for at least 5 minutes before serving garnished with scallions (if using)

Helpful Hack: For an easy and tidy way to scoop out the tender insides of the potatoes, use an ice cream scoop.

Per serving: Calories: 412; Total Fat: 25g; Saturated Fat: 12g; Cholesterol: 64mg; Carbohydrates: 36g; Fiber: 3g; Sodium: 403mg; Protein: 14g

Loaded Nachos

Prep time: 15 minutes **Cook time:** 20 minutes

Nachos are quick and easy to put together and serve while watching all those sports games and during all of the family activities that busy weekends bring. These loaded nachos turn boring snacks into cheesy, crunchy finger food that will be scooped up in just seconds. You might be smart to double the recipe. **Serves 6**

1 tablespoon olive oil

1 pound ground beef, chicken, or turkey

1 packet gluten-free taco seasoning

Crispy Tortilla Chips (page 44) to fill the bottom of a baking sheet (4 to 5 handfuls)

3 cups shredded Colby Jack or Cheddar cheese

½ cup chopped tomatoes

¼ cup chopped sweet onion

2 tablespoons chopped scallions, both green and white parts

½ cup diced bell pepper

¼ cup chopped fresh cilantro leaves

1. Preheat the broiler to low.

2. In a large nonstick skillet, heat the oil. Add the meat and taco seasoning and cook according to the taco seasoning packet's instructions, for 5 to 10 minutes, depending on the meat you have chosen. Remove from the heat.

3. Fill the bottom of a large rimmed baking sheet with tortilla chips. Add the cooked meat and then the cheese evenly on top of the chips.

4. Sprinkle the tomatoes, onion, scallions, and bell pepper on top.

5. Broil for 4 to 8 minutes, or until the cheese has melted and the outside chips and cheese turn golden brown.

6. Remove from the oven and immediately sprinkle with the cilantro. Allow to cool for a few minutes, and serve while the cheese is still stringy and melty.

- -

Per serving: Calories: 440; Total Fat: 30g; Saturated Fat: 14g; Cholesterol: 107mg; Carbohydrates: 12g; Fiber: 1g; Sodium: 580mg; Protein: 30g

Quick al Fresco Bruschetta

Prep time: 5 minutes **Cook time:** 5 minutes

One of my all-time favorites, this recipe is extremely easy to put together. Toasting the garlic bread pieces fills the entire home with a warm, inviting garlic smell. The fresh seasoned vegetable topping is addictively good, and the last bites are always followed with finger licking. That's when you know it's good. **Serves 12**

FOR THE BRUSCHETTA

1 small loaf sliced gluten-free bread, slices halved
3 tablespoons unsalted butter at room temperature
2 tablespoons Italian seasoning
Pinch salt

FOR THE TOPPING

7 to 8 roma tomatoes, diced
⅓ red onion, diced
1 tablespoon minced garlic
2 tablespoons olive oil
1 tablespoon balsamic vinegar
Salt
Freshly ground black pepper
8 to 10 fresh basil leaves, chopped

TO MAKE THE BRUSCHETTA

1. Preheat the broiler to high.

2. Lay the bread slice halves on a baking sheet. Lightly butter the tops and evenly sprinkle with the Italian seasoning and salt. (You may need to cook the toast in batches, depending on the size of the baking sheet and oven.)

3. Broil for 2 to 4 minutes, removing immediately once the edges have turned golden brown and the bread pieces have hardened slightly to a toast consistency. Do not overcook.

TO MAKE THE TOPPING

4. In a large bowl, combine the tomatoes, onion, garlic, oil, and vinegar and season with salt and pepper.

5. Place a spoonful of the topping on each piece of toast. Serve garnished with the basil.

Per serving: Calories: 141; Total Fat: 6g; Saturated Fat: 2g; Cholesterol: 8mg; Carbohydrates: 19g; Fiber: 2g; Sodium: 198mg; Protein: 4g

Spiced Roasted Nuts

Prep time: 5 minutes **Cook time:** 30 minutes

This simple recipe results in handfuls of addictive, irresistibly sweet and spicy roasted nuts. It is perfect for tailgating and holiday parties. **Makes 3 cups**

3 cups nuts of choice
2 tablespoons unsalted butter, melted
2 tablespoons hot sauce
1 tablespoon packed light brown sugar
¼ teaspoon garlic powder
Pinch sea salt

1. Preheat the oven to 250°F. Line a baking sheet with parchment paper.

2. In a large bowl, combine the nuts, butter, hot sauce, sugar, and garlic powder and stir well to coat evenly.

3. Spread the nuts in a single layer on the prepared baking sheet and cook for 15 minutes.

4. Remove the baking sheet, stir and flip the nuts, sprinkle with the salt, and bake for another 10 to 15 minutes, or until the nuts are toasted.

5. Remove from the oven and allow to cool before enjoying.

Ingredient Swap: If you don't like spicy foods, you can still enjoy this recipe by substituting your favorite gluten-free barbecue sauce for the hot sauce.

Per serving (½ cup): Calories: 386; Total Fat: 40g; Saturated Fat: 5g; Cholesterol: 10mg; Carbohydrates: 9g; Fiber: 5g; Sodium: 87mg; Protein: 5g

Zucchini Bites

Prep time: 5 minutes **Cook time:** 2 minutes

Zucchini bites are one of my family's favorite recipes for parties and watching sports. I love it because these bite-size finger foods are totally tasty and take just minutes to make from start to finish with minimal cleanup afterward. With this dish, everybody wins. **Makes 16 pieces**

½ cup shredded parmesan cheese
¼ cup gluten-free mayonnaise
½ teaspoon dried basil
1 medium zucchini, cut into ⅓-inch rounds

1. Preheat the broiler to low. Line a baking sheet with aluminum foil.

2. In a small bowl, stir together the cheese, mayonnaise, and basil until well combined.

3. Place each zucchini slice flat on the prepared baking sheet. Spread the cheese mixture evenly over all the zucchini slices.

4. Broil for 1 to 2 minutes, or until the cheesy tops turn golden brown. Remove from the oven. Allow to cool for 2 to 3 minutes before serving.

Ingredient Swap: This recipe is a great one to experiment with. Substitute thyme or Italian seasoning for the basil. Like spice? Add some red pepper flakes to the mix. The variations are endless with this insanely easy recipe.

Per serving (1 bite): Calories: 39; Total Fat: 3g; Saturated Fat: 1g; Cholesterol: 4mg; Carbohydrates: 1g; Fiber: 0g; Sodium: 79mg; Protein: 1g

Cheesy Flatbread

Prep time: 15 minutes **Cook time:** 15 minutes

This delicious finger food uses an easy and fast gluten-free crust that is baked partway before cheesy toppings are added. Then it's back into the already-hot oven to finish off the dish. Your kitchen will smell amazing, and your palate will be more than pleased. **Serves 4**

Gluten-free cooking spray, for coating the baking sheet

1¾ cups gluten-free all-purpose flour

½ teaspoon salt

½ teaspoon xanthan gum

1 package rapid/instant yeast

½ cup milk of choice

2 tablespoons unsalted butter, at room temperature

1 large egg, at room temperature, beaten

1 tablespoon honey

½ teaspoon apple cider vinegar

1 cup chopped fresh spinach

2 tablespoons gluten-free pesto

2 cups shredded mozzarella cheese

1. Preheat the oven to 450°F. Spray a large nonstick baking sheet with cooking spray.

2. In the bowl of a stand mixer or a large bowl, combine the flour, salt, and xanthan gum.

3. Make a small hole with your finger in the middle of the flour mixture and pour the yeast into that hole.

4. Warm the milk to around 115°F in the microwave, using a thermometer to check the temperature, usually 30 to 45 seconds on high power. Pour the warm milk over the yeast.

5. Add the butter, egg, honey, and vinegar to the bowl and mix using the dough hook attachment on the mixer or a handheld mixer for about 2 minutes, or until fully combined.

6. Using your hands sprayed with cooking spray, place the dough on the prepared baking sheet and flatten it out into a ¼-inch-thick rectangle.

7. Bake on the middle rack of the oven for 6 minutes, then remove it. Sprinkle the spinach on top of the dough, drizzle with the pesto, and top with the cheese.

8. Return it to the oven for 4 to 5 minutes, or until the cheese has melted and is turning golden brown around the edges. Remove from the oven.

Per serving: Calories: 487; Total Fat: 25g; Saturated Fat: 13g; Cholesterol: 110mg; Carbohydrates: 53g; Fiber: 1g; Sodium: 698mg; Protein: 20g

Mini Corn Dogs

Prep time: 10 minutes **Cook time:** 5 minutes

There is now no need to keep holding on to that craving for state fair–style corn dogs. You can have delicious gluten-free mini corn dogs in minutes, without even leaving the house. Pieces of your favorite hot dogs or sausages are dipped into a thick corn-based batter and then quickly fried to golden brown perfection, giving you bite after bite of corn dog bliss. **Serves 8**

Cooking oil, for frying
½ cup gluten-free cornmeal
1 cup gluten-free Bisquick
  mix or Homemade
  Gluten-Free Baking Mix
  (page 13), divided
1 tablespoon sugar
1 large egg, beaten
⅔ cup milk of choice
4 regular-size gluten-free hot
  dogs, partially cooked or
  heated in microwave for
  30 seconds then halved
Sticks, (optional)

1. Line a plate with paper towels. In a wok or saucepan, heat 2 to 3 inches of oil over medium heat.

2. In a medium bowl, combine the cornmeal, ¾ cup of baking mix, and the sugar and stir. Stir in the egg and milk. Pour the remaining ¼ cup of baking mix into a small bowl and add the hot dog pieces to coat.

3. Dip the dusted hot dog pieces in the batter and patiently cover all sides. The batter may not want to stick to the hot dog at first.

4. Drop each battered hot dog piece into the hot oil and cook for 2 to 3 minutes, flipping once, or until the batter fluffs up and turns golden brown. Quickly remove them from the oil with a large fork or vented spatula and put them on the plate to cool.

Prep Tip: For best results, allow the batter to rest for 2 to 3 minutes before rolling the hot dogs in it. This will give the dry and wet ingredients time to work together to create the best performing batter.

Per serving: Calories: 243; Total Fat: 14g; Saturated Fat: 4g; Cholesterol: 42mg; Carbohydrates: 24g; Fiber: 1g; Sodium: 482mg; Protein: 6g

Garlic Cheese Rolls

Prep time: 10 minutes **Cook time:** 10 minutes

Don't worry about missing out on one of dinner's most important components: the dinner roll. These soft and moist garlic cheese rolls will be a new gluten-free dinner table favorite in no time. On top of packing a deliciously garlicky punch, the rolls are incredibly quick and easy to put together, making them perfect for busy weeknight meals. **Serves 12 to 16**

FOR THE CHEESE ROLLS

2½ cups shredded mozzarella cheese
½ cup white rice flour
1 ounce cream cheese, at room temperature
1 large egg
1 teaspoon baking soda

FOR THE GARLIC BUTTER TOPPING

1½ teaspoons minced garlic
3 tablespoons salted butter, melted
2 teaspoons chopped fresh basil leaves
2 tablespoons grated parmesan cheese

TO MAKE THE CHEESE ROLLS

1. Preheat the oven to 400°F. Line a baking sheet with parchment paper.

2. In a food processor, combine the mozzarella cheese, rice flour, cream cheese, egg, and baking soda and pulse until mixed thoroughly. Remove the dough from the food processor and knead with your hands until smooth.

3. Rolling the dough between your hands, creating balls the size of a ping-pong ball. Shape them into domes and place them 2 inches apart on the prepared baking sheet. Bake for 5 to 7 minutes, or until the tops turn golden brown. Remove from the oven to cool.

TO MAKE THE GARLIC BUTTER TOPPING

4. In a small bowl, stir together the garlic, butter, basil, and parmesan cheese. Brush or spoon the butter on top of each cheese roll.

Per serving: Calories: 138; Total Fat: 10g; Saturated Fat: 6g; Cholesterol: 45mg; Carbohydrates: 6g; Fiber: 0g; Sodium: 304mg; Protein: 7g

Pepperoni Pizza Bites

Prep time: 10 minutes **Cook time:** 10 minutes

As a kid, I remember many snack options of pizza bagels and pizza rollups. Now, as an adult on a gluten-free diet, I have come up with a sophisticated option for whenever I crave these childhood favorites. These pizza bites are customizable to your liking, but don't forget your childhood roots—add that tasty pepperoni. **Makes 12 pieces**

FOR THE PIZZA CRUST
2½ cups mozzarella cheese, shredded
½ cup white rice flour
1 ounce cream cheese, at room temperature
1 large egg
1 teaspoon baking soda

FOR ASSEMBLING THE INDIVIDUAL PIZZA BITES
1 teaspoon gluten-free pizza sauce
1 pepperoni, chopped
Pinch Italian seasoning
1 to 2 tablespoons shredded mozzarella cheese

TO MAKE THE PIZZA CRUST

1. Preheat the oven to 400°F. Line a baking sheet with parchment paper.

2. In a food processor, combine the mozzarella cheese, flour, cream cheese, egg, and baking soda and pulse until mixed thoroughly. Remove from the food processor and knead with your hands until a smooth dough forms.

3. Rolling the dough between your hands, create balls the size of a ping-pong ball and place them 2 inches apart on the prepared baking sheet. Press down on each dough ball until it is ½ to ¾ inch thick. Bake for 5 to 7 minutes, or until the top of each crust turns golden brown. Remove from the oven to cool.

4. Flip each crust over so that the flat bottom is now facing up. Spoon the pizza sauce in an even layer on each crust. Add the pepperoni, Italian seasoning, and mozzarella cheese. Place the pizza bites back on the baking sheet and bake for another 2 to 3 minutes, or until the cheese has melted. Remove from the oven. Allow to cool for 2 to 3 minutes, and serve while still warm.

Ingredient Swap: These pizza bites are completely customizable. If you are a cheese pizza person or want a vegetarian option, don't add the pepperoni. Want sausage and green pepper pizza? Add it, making sure to use precooked meat because these pizza bites don't spend enough time in the oven to fully cook any uncooked meat.

Per serving (1 pizza bite): Calories: 125; Total Fat: 8g; Saturated Fat: 4g; Cholesterol: 40mg; Carbohydrates: 6g; Fiber: 0g; Sodium: 328mg; Protein: 7g

Easy Chicken Noodle Soup, page 64

CHAPTER 5

Soups, Salads, and Sides

Easy Chicken Noodle Soup

Prep time: 5 minutes **Cook time:** 20 minutes

This super-quick, one-pot, warm, and herby chicken noodle soup is comfort in every spoonful. I like to use either spaghetti or fettuccine, although kids love the spiral-looking rotini when you want to mix it up a bit. **Serves 6**

2 tablespoons cooking oil, plus more as needed
½ medium onion, chopped
2 teaspoons minced garlic
1 cup chopped celery
1 medium carrot, chopped
10 thyme sprigs
2 teaspoons dried oregano
½ teaspoon salt
¼ teaspoon freshly ground black pepper
8 cups chicken broth
3 cups cubed or shredded cooked chicken
10 ounces gluten-free pasta

1. In a large pot, heat the oil, onion, and garlic over medium heat. Sauté for about 5 minutes, or until the onion becomes golden brown and fragrant.

2. Add the celery, carrot, thyme, oregano, salt, and pepper and cook for 1 minute while stirring. If the ingredients start to stick to the bottom of the pot, add a dash more oil.

3. Add the broth and chicken and bring to a boil. Once boiling, add the pasta and cook according to the package instructions. Remove from the heat.

4. Serve in big bowls, sprinkled with your favorite soup toppings.

Something Extra: The best toppings for this soup are fresh thyme leaves, a sprinkling of shredded cheese, and the garlic toasts from the Quick al Fresco Bruschetta (page 53) for dipping.

Per serving: Calories: 445; Total Fat: 12g; Saturated Fat: 2g; Cholesterol: 62mg; Carbohydrates: 52g; Fiber: 6g; Sodium: 710mg; Protein: 31g

NUT-FREE

Wild Rice Soup

Prep time: 30 minutes **Cook time:** 20 minutes

My grandmother was one amazing cook, and I have the best memories of visiting her Minnesota home, walking into a house full of the most amazing aromas of creamy, savory comforts. This soup recipe is from her stockpile of incredible recipes. There is nothing more comforting than your grand-mother's favorite soup, especially one that is gluten-free. **Serves 6 to 8**

½ cup wild rice
6 tablespoons unsalted butter
¼ cup chopped onion
¼ cup finely chopped celery
6 tablespoons white
    rice flour
¼ teaspoon salt
¼ teaspoon freshly ground
    black pepper
¼ teaspoon ground allspice
2 cups chicken broth
1 cup cream

1. Cook the rice according to the package instructions.

2. While the rice is cooking, in a large nonstick skil-let, heat the butter over medium-low heat. Add the onion and celery and sauté for 3 to 4 minutes, or until the onion is translucent and tender.

3. Reduce the heat to low and stir in the flour, salt, pepper, and allspice. Continue to stir until the mixture starts to bubble. Add the broth, continuously stirring until boiling. Stir and let boil for 1 minute.

4. Stir in the cream and cooked rice and simmer for 5 to 10 minutes, stirring occasionally. Remove from the heat and allow to cool for 3 to 5 minutes before serving.

- -

Something Extra: This soup is insanely delicious topped with bacon bits and shredded cheese. Want even more protein? Add cooked chopped or shredded chicken pieces to the soup when you are adding the cream and rice during the final 5 to 10 minutes of simmering.

- -

Per serving: Calories: 347; Total Fat: 27g; Saturated Fat: 16g; Cholesterol: 87mg; Carbohydrates: 21g; Fiber: 1g; Sodium: 322mg; Protein: 6g

Lasagna Soup

Prep time: 5 minutes **Cook time:** 25 minutes

Lasagna is traditionally made with a lot of gluten, however, there's none in this twist on the comfort food. Plus, you can enjoy the aromas and flavors of lasagna with the warm comforts of a big bowl of soup and there's only one pot to clean up. Serve with Quick al Fresco Bruschetta (page 53).

Serves 8

1 tablespoon unsalted
   butter or olive oil
1 sweet onion, diced
1½ tablespoons
   minced garlic
1½ pounds ground beef,
   ground turkey, or
   ground chicken
3 tablespoons Italian
   seasoning
1 (24-ounce) jar gluten-free
   spaghetti sauce
4 cups chicken or beef broth
1 (15-ounce) can crushed
   tomatoes
¾ cup heavy cream
10 to 12 ounces gluten-free
   lasagna noodles, broken
   into 1- to 2-inch pieces
1½ cups shredded mozza-
   rella cheese
1 cup ricotta cheese
Chopped fresh basil leaves
   and grated parmesan
   cheese, for garnish
   (optional)

1. In a large Dutch oven, heat the butter, onion, and garlic over medium-high heat for 3 to 4 minutes, or until they turn soft and fragrant. Add the ground beef and Italian seasoning and cook for about 8 minutes, or until the meat is fully cooked with no pink.

2. Add the spaghetti sauce, broth, crushed tomatoes, and cream. Stir and bring to a simmer. Add the lasagna noodles and cook for 8 to 10 minutes, or until al dente.

3. Once the pasta has cooked, add the mozzarella cheese and ricotta cheese and stir until melted. Remove from the heat, garnish with basil and par-mesan cheese (if using), and serve warm.

4. Store room-temperature leftovers in an airtight con-tainer in the refrigerator for up to 3 days.

Per serving: Calories: 542; Total Fat: 26g; Saturated Fat: 14g; Cholesterol: 153mg; Carbohydrates: 41g; Fiber: 4g; Sodium: 869mg; Protein: 37g

Sesame-Ginger Chicken Chopped Salad

Prep time: 10 minutes

This light, refreshing salad tossed in a flavor-packed sesame-ginger dressing will add a zing to anyone's meal. If you are looking for a great meal-prepping dish or a fast, delightful lunch on the go, this recipe is it.

Serves 6 to 8

---

2 tablespoons liquid aminos or gluten-free soy sauce

3 tablespoons gluten-free sweet chili paste

2 tablespoons sesame oil

2 tablespoons coconut aminos

¼ teaspoon ground ginger

3 cups diced or shredded cooked chicken

2 tablespoons white-wine vinegar

1 head lettuce, chopped

2 cups chopped vegetables of choice (such as peas, carrots, onions, mushrooms, etc.)

1. In a medium bowl, combine the liquid aminos, chili paste, oil, coconut aminos, and ginger, then transfer half of the mixture to a separate bowl. Add the chicken to half of the marinade and refrigerate.

2. Add the vinegar to the remaining marinade to make the dressing and mix well.

3. Put the lettuce and vegetables in a large serving bowl. Add the marinated chicken and then drizzle with the dressing. Toss to combine. Chill in the refrigerator until ready to serve.

- -

Serving Tip: I like to add some crunch to the top of this delicious salad. Almond pieces; crisp, fresh sliced scallions (green parts only); or sesame seeds add a great crunch without any croutons.

- -

Per serving: Calories: 175; Total Fat: 8g; Saturated Fat: 1g; Cholesterol: 53mg; Carbohydrates: 5g; Fiber: 2g; Sodium: 482mg; Protein: 21g

Lime-Chipotle Corn Salad

Prep time: 5 minutes

Just five short minutes will produce this perfect side dish or party food. This salad is refreshingly juicy and packed with nutrients. The zingy dressing makes this dish stand out even more than its brilliant colors. **Serves 8**

3 (15-ounce) cans sweet corn kernels, drained

8 small-medium radishes, very thinly sliced

½ sweet red onion, chopped

¼ cup chopped fresh Italian parsley

¼ cup freshly squeezed lime juice (2 to 3 small limes)

¼ cup olive oil

½ teaspoon ground coriander

½ teaspoon chipotle chile powder

½ teaspoon garlic powder

¼ teaspoon freshly ground black pepper

¼ teaspoon coarse salt

1. In a large bowl, combine the corn, radishes, onion, and parsley.

2. In a medium bowl, combine the lime juice, oil, coriander, chile powder, garlic powder, pepper, and salt and stir thoroughly to make the dressing.

3. Pour the dressing over the corn and radish mixture and stir until well coated. Chill in the refrigerator until ready to serve.

Helpful Hack: This is a great recipe for parties and get togethers. Double or triple this recipe to easily feed a crowd. The salad chills very well, so feel free to make it ahead of time.

Per serving: Calories: 114; Total Fat: 8g; Saturated Fat: 1g; Cholesterol: 0mg; Carbohydrates: 12g; Fiber: 2g; Sodium: 196mg; Protein: 2g

Flash-Fried Green Beans

Prep time: 5 minutes **Cook time:** 10 minutes

There are few things better than quickly prepared dark-green vegetable side dishes on the dinner table. This easy green bean recipe will have the whole family licking their plates clean. **Serves 4**

2 tablespoons sesame oil or cooking oil of choice
1 pound green beans, trimmed
¼ cup chopped onion
1 teaspoon minced garlic
Salt
Freshly ground black pepper

In a large skillet, heat the oil over medium heat and then add the green beans. Sauté, stirring occasionally, for 2 minutes. Add the onion and garlic and cook for another 5 to 7 minutes, depending on how tender you like the green beans. Remove from the heat, season with salt and pepper, and serve.

Something Extra: You can easily turn this dish into a teriyaki green bean dish. Combine 1 tablespoon honey, 1 tablespoon gluten-free soy sauce (or coconut aminos), 1 teaspoon rice vinegar, and 1 teaspoon coconut sugar (or granulated sugar) in a small bowl and pour over the sautéing beans during the final 3 to 4 minutes of cooking.

Per serving: Calories: 100; Total Fat: 7g; Saturated Fat: 1g; Cholesterol: 0mg; Carbohydrates: 9g; Fiber: 3g; Sodium: 46mg; Protein: 2g

Grilled Caesar Salad

Prep time: 10 minutes **Cook time:** 1 minute

If you need a fun spin on an old classic, a delicious Caesar salad, with home-made dressing drizzled over fresh grilled lettuce leaves, may be just what you have been waiting for. Add your favorite toppings sprinkled on top and grill up your favorite protein while the grill is lit and hot. There's no better healthy combination. **Serves 2**

1 head romaine lettuce
2 tablespoons olive oil
¼ cup gluten-free croutons
¼ cup crumbled cheese
¼ cup cooked bacon
  crumbles
Freshly ground black pepper
½ cup plain nonfat
  Greek yogurt
1½ tablespoons freshly
  squeezed lemon juice
2 garlic cloves
⅓ cup grated parme-
  san cheese
1 teaspoon anchovy paste
1 teaspoon Dijon mustard

1. Preheat the grill to high heat.

2. Split the lettuce in half, hot dog–style. Wash the lettuce and allow to dry completely before starting the cooking process.

3. Gently brush the inside of each lettuce half with 1 tablespoon of oil. Put the lettuce heads (insides down) on the grill for about 30 seconds. There will be grill marks and the edges will start to brown. Remove from the heat. Transfer to a serving dish.

4. Pile the croutons, cheese, and bacon crumbles on the grilled lettuce. Season with pepper.

5. In a food processor, combine the yogurt, lemon juice, garlic, parmesan cheese, anchovy paste, and mustard. Season with pepper. Blend the ingredients until smooth. Pour the dressing over the salad.

Variation Tip: Grilled chicken, pork, and shrimp go great with grilled Caesar salad. My family's favorite garnishes for this dish include black pepper, gluten-free croutons, extra cheese, and bacon crumbles.

Per serving: Calories: 488; Total Fat: 35g; Saturated Fat: 10g; Cholesterol: 56mg; Carbohydrates: 20g; Fiber: 7g; Sodium: 950mg; Protein: 27g

ONE POT, NUT-FREE, LOW-CARB, VEGAN

Vegetable Stew

Prep time: 10 minutes **Cook time:** 55 minutes

Nothing is more comforting than a big bowl of stew, especially when every stir brings that savory aroma of home cooking. This recipe is a triple winner: it's made in just one pot, is mostly hands-off, and serves a large crowd. Yes!

Serves 10 to 12

3 tablespoons olive oil

1 sweet onion, chopped

2 tablespoons minced garlic

2 teaspoons salt

1 teaspoon freshly ground black pepper

1 large or 2 medium potatoes, peeled and diced

1 cup sliced or diced carrots

1 (15-ounce) can sweet corn, drained

1 cup fresh or frozen peas

1 cup chopped green beans

1 cup diced tomatoes

1 (6-ounce) can tomato paste

5 cups vegetable broth

1. In a Dutch oven or large stock pot or saucepot, heat the oil, onion, and garlic. Cook for 3 to 4 minutes, or until tender and fragrant. Add the salt, pepper, potatoes, carrots, corn, peas, green beans, tomatoes, tomato paste, and broth. Stir and bring to a simmer.

2. Simmer for 45 to 50 minutes, stirring occasionally. Remove from the heat and let cool for 5 minutes before serving.

Prep Tip: If you like stew a little on the creamy side, add ¾ cup cream or 1 cup shredded cheese to the stew during the final 10 minutes of simmering and stir occasionally.

Per serving: Calories: 126; Total Fat: 5g; Saturated Fat: 1g; Cholesterol: 0mg; Carbohydrates: 20g; Fiber: 4g; Sodium: 521mg; Protein: 3g

White Chicken Chili

Prep time: 5 minutes **Cook time:** 55 minutes

Stick-to-your-ribs, easy stovetop chili is a delicious and comforting meal in a bowl. This low-carb chili is made in just one pot. And it's really tasty.

Serves 6

3 to 4 cups chopped cooked chicken

4 cups water

1 cup milk

1 cup chopped onion

1 (15-ounce) can sweet corn kernels

½ cup masa flour mixed with ½ cup water

2 tablespoons paprika

1 tablespoon freshly ground black pepper

½ tablespoon salt

1 tablespoon minced garlic

1 tablespoon ground cumin

1 tablespoon dried oregano

12 ounces shredded Monterey Jack cheese

1. In a Dutch oven or large saucepan, combine the chicken, water, milk, onion, corn, flour mixture, paprika, pepper, salt, garlic, cumin, and oregano over medium heat. Stir well.

2. Bring the mixture to a simmer and cook for 45 minutes, stirring occasionally.

3. Stir in the cheese and simmer for an additional 10 minutes, stirring occasionally. Remove from the heat and allow to cool for 5 minutes before topping with your favorite garnishes and enjoying.

Helpful Hack: Have a little extra time to let this dish simmer all day in a slow cooker? Simply combine all the ingredients except for the shredded cheese in the slow cooker and stir. Cook on low for 10 to 12 hours or on high for 5 to 6 hours. Stir in the shredded cheese during the final 30 minutes of cooking. Allow to cool for 3 to 5 minutes before serving.

Per serving: Calories: 460; Total Fat: 23g; Saturated Fat: 12g; Cholesterol: 107mg; Carbohydrates: 27g; Fiber: 3g; Sodium: 1,202mg; Protein: 37g

Sweet Poppy Seed Salad

Prep time: 5 minutes

This dressing is swift, sweet, and tangy—the perfect salad dressing to drizzle on top of everything, not just salads. Don't be tempted to omit the pumpkin; this unusual ingredient adds depth to every pour. **Serves 4 to 6**

⅓ cup distilled white vinegar
¼ cup maple syrup
⅛ teaspoon salt
½ teaspoon minced garlic
½ cup olive oil
¼ cup pumpkin puree
2 teaspoons poppy seeds
1 pound lettuce of choice

1. In a blender, combine the vinegar, maple syrup, salt, garlic, oil, and pumpkin and blend until thoroughly combined. Stir in the poppy seeds.

2. Drizzle the dressing over the lettuce, your favorite tossed salad, chopped salad, or chicken salad and all your favorite fixings. Store in an airtight container in the refrigerator for up to 5 days.

Prep Tip: Don't stir the poppy seeds into the dressing until after all other ingredients have been well blended. You'll want that extra crunch from the poppy seeds to stay intact. That little extra texture is beautiful and delicious.

Per serving: Calories: 321; Total Fat: 28g; Saturated Fat: 4g; Cholesterol: 0mg; Carbohydrates: 17g; Fiber: 2g; Sodium: 88mg; Protein: 2g

Balsamic Brussels Sprouts

Prep time: 5 minutes **Cook time:** 30 minutes

If you have been looking for a gourmet recipe without the gourmet price tag or expertise, this is the one for you. These Brussels sprouts are an easy side dish full of sweet, hearty flavors. The sprouts are roasted in lemon juice and olive oil before being drizzled with a bacon-pecan reduction and then quickly roasted again. **Serves 4**

3 cups halved Brussels
   sprouts
2 tablespoons olive oil
1 teaspoon freshly squeezed
   lemon juice
Salt
Freshly ground black pepper
¼ cup balsamic vinegar
2 tablespoons honey
2 tablespoons finely
   chopped bacon (in food
   processor), plus more
   for garnish
2 tablespoons finely
   chopped pecans (in food
   processor), plus more
   for garnish

1. Preheat the oven to 400°F. Line a rimmed baking sheet with aluminum foil.

2. Spread the sprouts out on the prepared baking sheet and evenly coat with the oil and lemon juice. Season with salt and pepper. Bake for 15 minutes.

3. Meanwhile, in a small saucepan, combine the vinegar, honey, bacon, and pecans. Bring to a simmer over medium heat and cook until the liquid is about half its original volume. Remove from the heat.

4. Remove the sprouts from the oven and stir. Drizzle the sauce on top and roast for another 10 to 15 minutes. Remove from the oven.

5. Serve garnished with bacon and pecans.

Variation Tip: This side dish is spectacular with goat cheese, blue cheese, or Gorgonzola crumbles and the nuts of your choice.

Per serving: Calories: 183; Total Fat: 11g; Saturated Fat: 2g; Cholesterol: 6mg; Carbohydrates: 18g; Fiber: 3g; Sodium: 156mg; Protein: 5g

Creamy Broccoli Salad

Prep time: 5 minutes

This broccoli salad is a simple veggie dish that combines sweetness and creaminess. This version uses Greek yogurt to keep the creaminess and add some lightness. It's the perfect healthy side dish for any meal where time is short and appetites are big. **Serves 8**

¼ cup plain Greek yogurt

3 tablespoons sugar

1 tablespoon white-wine vinegar

3 small heads broccoli, cut into bite-size florets

1 medium red onion, chopped

3 tablespoons sun-flower seeds

½ cup dried cranberries

⅓ cup crumbled or chopped bacon

1. In a small bowl, combine the yogurt, sugar, and vinegar thoroughly.

2. In a large bowl, combine the broccoli, onion, sunflower seeds, cranberries, and bacon.

3. Drizzle the dressing over the salad and toss until evenly coated. Serve immediately or chill in the refrigerator until ready to eat.

Per serving: Calories: 147; Total Fat: 6g; Saturated Fat: 2g; Cholesterol: 12mg; Carbohydrates: 19g; Fiber: 3g; Sodium: 182mg; Protein: 7g

Au Gratin Potatoes

Prep time: 10 minutes **Cook time:** 50 minutes

With just eight ingredients that are likely staples in your kitchen, it'll be easy for you to have this must-have potato dish for the next family dinner. In fact, this dish is my go-to when I haven't been to the grocery store in a while, since I always have these ingredients on hand. **Serves 8**

Gluten-free cooking spray or unsalted butter, for greasing

5 medium or 4 large Russet potatoes, peeled and cut into 1-inch cubes

1½ tablespoons garlic powder

1 teaspoon salt

½ teaspoon freshly ground black pepper, plus pinch

1 cup grated parmesan cheese, divided

2 cups heavy cream, divided

Chopped fresh rosemary or thyme leaves, for garnish

1. Preheat the oven to 350°F. Grease a 2-quart baking dish with cooking spray.

2. In a medium bowl, combine the potatoes, garlic powder, salt, and ½ teaspoon of pepper. Mix well.

3. Cover the bottom of the dish with one-fourth of the potatoes and then sprinkle ¼ cup of cheese evenly on top of the potatoes. Pour ½ cup of cream on top of the cheese.

4. Repeat step 3 three more times, totaling 4 layers.

5. Sprinkle with a pinch of pepper and bake for 50 minutes, until the edges are golden brown and bubbling. Remove from the oven and let it set for 5 to 7 minutes to thicken up and cool down. Garnish with rosemary and serve warm.

Prep Tip: You can easily turn this dish into scalloped potatoes by cutting the potatoes into slices or "coins" and creating a single layer of potato slices, each slice slightly overlapping the previous one.

Per serving: Calories: 164; Total Fat: 4g; Saturated Fat: 2g; Cholesterol: 11mg; Carbohydrates: 27g; Fiber: 2g; Sodium: 524mg; Protein: 7g

Creamy Pasta Salad

Prep time: 10 minutes **Cook time:** 10 minutes

The freshness of crisp vegetables combines with cool, tangy, creamy gluten-free pasta for this swift and easy salad. Its simplicity and fast prep makes this the perfect make-ahead dish for backyard barbecues and quick weeknight meals. Simply mix it together and chill it in the refrigerator until you're ready to dish it up. Couldn't be easier. Use dairy-free cheese crumbles to make the dish dairy-free. **Serves 8**

10 ounces gluten-free pasta

¼ cup olive oil

½ to ¾ cup feta cheese crumbles

3 tablespoons red-wine vinegar

1 tablespoon minced garlic

2 teaspoons dried oregano

½ teaspoon garlic powder

½ teaspoon onion powder

1 cup diced cucumber

2 cups grape tomatoes, sliced

½ red onion, diced

2 cups chopped bell pepper

1. Cook the pasta until al dente according to the package directions. Drain and rinse in cool water, transfer to a bowl, and immediately mix with the oil. Set aside in the refrigerator to cool.

2. In a small bowl, combine the cheese, vinegar, garlic, oregano, garlic powder, and onion powder. Mix with the pasta.

3. Add the cucumber, tomatoes, onion, and bell pepper and return to the refrigerator to cool further.

Something Extra: We turn this dish into a main meal on hot summer days or weeknights when we're short on time by having it ready to go, then grilling meat and adding to the cooled pasta salad when we're ready to eat.

Per serving: Calories: 234; Total Fat: 10g; Saturated Fat: 2g; Cholesterol: 8mg; Carbohydrates: 33g; Fiber: 5g; Sodium: 91mg; Protein: 5g

Wild Rice Pilaf

Prep time: 30 minutes **Cook time:** 40 minutes

Light and fluffy wild rice stirred around soft and tender vegetable pieces and seasoned with common spices makes for an easy and healthy side dish. Take it up a notch by toasting your favorite chopped nuts and sprinkling them on top for a bit of extra crunch and depth. **Serves 6 to 8**

1 cup wild rice blend

Vegetable broth (equal to the amount of water the rice package instructions call for)

2 tablespoons unsalted butter

½ sweet onion, chopped

1 tablespoon minced garlic

¾ cup chopped mushrooms

½ cup finely diced carrots

1 teaspoon Italian seasoning

¼ teaspoon salt

¼ teaspoon freshly ground black pepper

½ to ¾ cup chopped pecans

1. In a large saucepan or Dutch oven, cook the wild rice in the vegetable broth according to the package instructions (making sure to swap out the water for the equivalent amount of vegetable broth). The wild rice will likely need to simmer for 30 to 40 minutes, depending on the brand.

2. While the rice is cooking, in a medium skillet, melt the butter over medium heat. Add the onion and garlic and cook for 2 to 3 minutes, or until softened and fragrant. Add the mushrooms, carrots, Italian seasoning, salt, and pepper and stir to combine. Continue to cook for 5 to 7 minutes, or until the carrots are tender-firm. Remove from the heat.

3. Once the rice is fully cooked, stir in the cooked vegetables, followed by the pecans. Stir well and serve warm.

Per serving: Calories: 205; Total Fat: 11g; Saturated Fat: 3g; Cholesterol: 10mg; Carbohydrates: 24g; Fiber: 3g; Sodium: 107mg; Protein: 5g

Cold Peanut Noodle Bowls, page 89

Meatless Mains

Vegetable Risotto

Prep time: 5 minutes **Cook time:** 55 minutes

Risotto is a creamy, pasta-like dish that is actually made from rice, so it's naturally gluten-free. It does take some time to make risotto, so it's a great recipe for the weekend, but it's simple and soothing to make, and you can enjoy the enticing aroma while you stir. **Serves 4**

5 cups vegetable broth
2 tablespoons olive oil
3 tablespoons dried onion
1 tablespoon minced garlic
1 cup Arborio rice
⅔ cup chopped mushrooms
⅔ cup 1½-inch-long pieces
  asparagus
½ cup cubed fresh mozza-
  rella cheese
1 tablespoon fresh
  thyme leaves
Freshly ground black pepper

1. In a small saucepan, heat the broth over medium-low heat until it starts to simmer.

2. In a large skillet, heat the oil over medium heat for 1 to 2 minutes. Add the onion and garlic and cook for 1 to 2 minutes, or until brown and fragrant.

3. Reduce the heat to medium-low and add the rice. Stir to coat the rice in the oil. Add ½ cup of warm broth to the rice, stirring every minute or so. Once the broth has almost completely evaporated, add another ½ cup of broth. Continue in the same manner until just ½ cup of broth is left.

4. When the last ½ cup of broth is being added to the rice, stir in the mushrooms, asparagus, cheese, thyme, and pepper. Stir frequently until the cheese is completely melted. Serve immediately.

Cooking Technique: Risotto needs a little bit of attention while cooking. Make sure to add just ½ cup of broth at a time and keep a close eye on the risotto as it soaks up the broth.

Per serving: Calories: 395; Total Fat: 14g; Saturated Fat: 4g; Cholesterol: 20mg; Carbohydrates: 51g; Fiber: 2g; Sodium: 522mg; Protein: 15g

Veggie Fried Rice

Prep time: 5 minutes **Cook time:** 25 minutes

Everything tastes better when it's made from scratch in your own kitchen. This fried rice recipe is packed full of fresh veggies and is no exception. In just half an hour, you can have drool-worthy fried rice on your dining table. **Serves 4**

3 tablespoons sesame oil, divided

2 teaspoons minced garlic

½ sweet onion, chopped

3 cups chopped fresh vegetables or frozen vegetables

1¼ cups vegetable broth

1½ cups jasmine rice, rinsed

5 tablespoons gluten-free soy sauce or liquid or coconut aminos

1 teaspoon garlic powder

½ teaspoon ground ginger

2 large eggs, beaten

1. In a large nonstick skillet, heat 1 tablespoon of oil for 1 to 2 minutes. Add the garlic and onion and sauté, stirring frequently, for 1 to 3 minutes, or until fragrant and softened. Add the vegetables and cook for 5 to 7 minutes, or until tender. Remove from the skillet and set aside.

2. Pour the broth into the same skillet and bring to a simmer. Once simmering, add the rice, stir, and continue to simmer until the rice has absorbed all the liquid.

3. Stir the vegetables into the cooked rice. Add the soy sauce, garlic powder, ginger, and remaining 2 tablespoons of oil and stir until evenly coated.

4. Move the rice to the edges of the skillet and add the eggs to the center. Scramble the eggs until fluffy and cooked. Then stir the scrambled eggs into the rice and vegetables. Remove from the heat.

Per serving: Calories: 539; Total Fat: 14g; Saturated Fat: 3g; Cholesterol: 95mg; Carbohydrates: 85g; Fiber: 9g; Sodium: 834mg; Protein: 16g

Southwest Quinoa Casserole

Prep time: 5 minutes **Cook time:** 25 minutes

Because of its versatility, this is the perfect gluten-free comfort food. Enjoy this dish as a warm casserole, as a hearty dip with your favorite chips, rolled up in a tortilla for a quick enchilada, or tossed over a piece of chicken or a salad to add a burst of flavor. **Serves 6 to 8**

2 cups vegetable broth

2 cups corn kernels, drained (about 2 [15¼-ounce] cans)

2 cups salsa

1 cup quinoa

1 cup black beans

1 cup chopped bell pepper

1½ tablespoons chili powder

1 tablespoon freshly squeezed lime juice

1 teaspoon minced garlic

1½ teaspoons dried oregano

¼ teaspoon salt

½ teaspoon freshly ground black pepper

½ teaspoon ground cumin

1 cup shredded cheese (optional)

1. Preheat the oven to 350°F.

2. In an oven-safe Dutch oven or oven-safe large non-stick skillet, combine the broth, corn, salsa, quinoa, beans, bell pepper, chili powder, lime juice, garlic, oregano, salt, pepper, and cumin over medium heat, and stir until fully combined.

3. Simmer for 15 to 20 minutes, or until the liquid has been absorbed (this will depend on how thick you want the casserole to be).

4. Sprinkle on the cheese (if using) and put the casserole in the oven for 3 to 5 minutes, or until the cheese melts. Remove from the oven and allow to cool for 5 minutes before serving.

- -

Slow Cooker Hack: If you have a little extra time, make this recipe in a slow cooker to fill your house with warm savory aromas for hours and hours. Combine all the ingredients except for the shredded cheese in the slow cooker and stir well. Cook on high for 2½ to 3 hours or on low for 4 to 6 hours. During the final 15 minutes of cooking, sprinkle on the shredded cheese and put the lid back on the slow cooker to help melt it.

- -

Per serving: Calories: 248; Total Fat: 4g; Saturated Fat: 1g; Cholesterol: 2mg; Carbohydrates: 44g; Fiber: 9g; Sodium: 884mg; Protein: 12g

Garlic-Avocado Pasta

Prep time: 5 minutes **Cook time:** 10 minutes

The savory sauce for this pasta can be whipped up in mere seconds. Despite the quick prep, the end product provides hearty flavors in a deliciously light dish. It's perfect for lunch or dinner. **Serves 6 to 8**

12 ounces gluten-free spaghetti
2 ripe medium avocados, pitted and peeled
⅓ cup olive oil
¼ cup finely chopped fresh parsley
1 tablespoon minced garlic
Sliced tomatoes, for serving
Sea salt

1. Cook the spaghetti according to the package instructions.

2. While the spaghetti is cooking, put the avocados in a food processor and pulse until smooth.

3. In a medium skillet, heat the oil, parsley, and garlic over medium heat until the garlic starts to sizzle. Immediately remove the skillet from the heat. Spoon the avocados into the skillet and mix thoroughly (it will separate a bit).

4. Mix the sauce with the spaghetti immediately after draining it. Serve with tomato slices and a sprinkle of sea salt.

Something Extra: For some added protein, cooked chicken or steak goes really well with this pasta dish.

Per serving: Calories: 436; Total Fat: 23g; Saturated Fat: 4g; Cholesterol: 0mg; Carbohydrates: 54g; Fiber: 12g; Sodium: 32mg; Protein: 7g

Hidden Veggie Baked Mac and Cheese

Prep time: 5 minutes **Cook time:** 20 minutes

Parents think they're being sneakily clever when they serve this mac and cheese. Kids don't care about the hidden veggies (and might not even notice); all they know is that it's delicious. Everyone wins with this dish.

Serves 8

1 (10-ounce) bag frozen cauliflower rice

8 ounces gluten-free pasta (I recommend elbow-shape Ancient Harvest Corn, Brown Rice & Quinoa)

2½ tablespoons unsalted butter

2 tablespoons all-purpose gluten-free flour

1¼ cups milk of choice

½ teaspoon paprika

2 teaspoons garlic powder

Salt

Freshly ground black pepper

4 ounces cream cheese

2 cups shredded cheese

1 cup plain gluten-free bread crumbs

1. Preheat the broiler to high. Microwave the cauliflower rice according to the package instructions.

2. Bring a large saucepan of water to a rolling boil and cook the pasta for 4 minutes only, then drain it and run cold water over the pasta to prevent further cooking.

3. While the pasta is boiling, in a large oven-safe skillet, melt the butter over medium heat. Add the flour and stir continuously for 1 to 2 minutes, or until it becomes clumpy and fragrant. Slowly add the milk, stirring continuously for 2 to 3 minutes, or until a homogenous cream sauce forms.

4. Add the paprika, garlic powder, salt, pepper, and cream cheese and allow the cream cheese to melt. Add the shredded cheese and stir for about 2 minutes, or until just melted.

5. Pour the pasta and cauliflower rice into the cheese sauce and stir just enough to evenly coat the pasta with sauce. Sprinkle the bread crumbs on top and broil for 2 to 3 minutes, or until the bread crumbs start to become a deeper shade of golden brown. Remove from the oven. Allow to cool for 2 to 3 minutes before serving.

6. Store leftovers in an airtight container in the refrigerator for up to 4 days. To reheat, put the desired amount in a microwave-safe dish with a loose-fitting cover and microwave for 30 to 60 seconds, or until warm and steamy.

Prep Tip: If you want the mac and cheese to be rich, stringy, and gooey, I highly recommend 1 cup of the shredded cheese be mozzarella and the other 1 cup be a different cheese, such as Cheddar or Colby or Jack.

Per serving: Calories: 378; Total Fat: 21g; Saturated Fat: 11g; Cholesterol: 58mg; Carbohydrates: 36g; Fiber: 5g; Sodium: 363mg; Protein: 13g

Caprese Casserole Bake

Prep time: 15 minutes **Cook time:** 35 minutes

This easy cheesy quinoa casserole is quickly assembled then popped into the oven to meld the basil, garlic, and onion flavors together. The simple balsamic reduction drizzled on top of the interleaved tomato and mozzarella slices makes this dish a gluten-free weeknight masterpiece. **Serves 6**

Gluten-free cooking
  spray, for coating the
  casserole dish
2 cups cooked quinoa
1 tablespoon olive oil
½ red onion, diced
2 tablespoons minced garlic
¼ cup chopped fresh
  basil leaves
2 medium tomatoes, cut into
  ¼-inch-thick slices
8 ounces fresh part-skim
  mozzarella cheese, cut into
  ¼-inch-thick slices
¼ cup balsamic vinegar
Freshly ground black pepper

1. Preheat the oven to 400°F. Spray a casserole dish with cooking spray and put the quinoa in a medium bowl.

2. In a medium skillet, heat the oil over medium heat for 1 to 2 minutes. Add the onion and garlic and sauté for 2 to 3 minutes, or until fragrant and tender.

3. Stir the onion and garlic mixture and the basil into the quinoa and transfer the mixture to the casserole dish.

4. Lay tomato slices and mozzarella circles on top of the quinoa, alternating between the two.

5. Bake for 25 to 30 minutes, or until the cheese is bubbly and golden brown. Remove from the oven.

6. While the casserole is baking, in a small saucepan, heat the vinegar until it simmers. Simmer for 4 to 5 minutes, or until the liquid reduces and becomes thicker and syrupy. Remove from the heat.

7. Drizzle the reduction on top of the cooked casserole and garnish with pepper.

Per serving: Calories: 322; Total Fat: 14g; Saturated Fat: 6g; Cholesterol: 36mg; Carbohydrates: 29g; Fiber: 4g; Sodium: 366mg; Protein: 19g

Cold Peanut Noodle Bowls

Prep time: 5 minutes **Cook time:** 15 minutes

My family devours these noodle bowls every chance they get. And because this is such a quick dish to put together, they get the chance pretty often. Another plus is that it is great for either lunch or dinner and is excellent reheated for a meal-on-the-go. Try this one; the sauce is so fantastic that you won't be able to slurp up the noodles fast enough. **Serves 4**

12 ounces gluten-free
   spaghetti
2 tablespoons sesame oil or
   olive oil
3 tablespoons minced
   garlic, divided
½ cup chopped mushrooms
1 bell pepper, chopped
1 medium carrot, grated
1 cup chopped cabbage
½ cup smooth peanut butter
¼ cup coconut aminos or
   soy aminos
3 tablespoons honey
2 tablespoons freshly
   squeezed lime juice
2 tablespoons rice vinegar
¼ teaspoon ground ginger
½ cup chopped fresh
   cilantro leaves, plus more
   for garnish
½ cup diced scallions, both
   green and white parts
Chopped peanuts,
   for garnish

1. Cook the spaghetti until al dente according to the package instructions, drain, then rinse with cold water until cool to the touch. Keep the spaghetti submerged in cool water.

2. Meanwhile, in a medium skillet, heat the oil over medium heat for about 30 seconds, or until fragrant. Add 1 tablespoon of garlic and the mushrooms, stir, and cook for 2 to 3 minutes, or until the garlic is golden brown and the mushrooms start to soften. Add the bell pepper, carrot, and cabbage and cook, stirring occasionally, for 5 to 7 minutes, or until softened. Remove from the heat.

3. To make the sauce, in a medium bowl, combine the peanut butter, coconut aminos, honey, lime juice, vinegar, ginger, and remaining 2 tablespoons of garlic and stir well.

4. Drain the spaghetti, then add the vegetables and sauce. Fold in the cilantro and scallions. Garnish with cilantro and peanuts and serve.

Per serving: Calories: 658; Total Fat: 25g; Saturated Fat: 5g; Cholesterol: 0mg; Carbohydrates: 98g; Fiber: 13g; Sodium: 603mg; Protein: 17g

Pesto Spaghetti Squash Bake

Prep time: 10 minutes **Cook time:** 55 minutes

Apart from the ease of preparation and delicious taste of this squash bake, it can be made well ahead of time, making it a great candidate for a busy weeknight family dinner. I make this dish in the morning, pop it in the refrigerator (where it will be absolutely fine for up to 12 hours), and slide it into the oven when I get home at the end of the day. Dinner done; happy family. **Serves 6**

Gluten-free cooking spray, for coating the baking dish
1 medium to large spaghetti squash, halved
Olive oil, for drizzling
2 cups chopped broccoli florets
1 cup chopped fresh baby spinach
⅔ cup gluten-free pesto
1½ to 2 cups shredded mozzarella cheese

1. Preheat the oven to 350°F. Spray a 9-by-13-inch glass or ceramic baking dish with cooking spray.

2. Place the squash, cut sides up, in the baking dish. Drizzle with olive oil and bake for about 40 minutes, or until the center is tender. Remove from the oven. Allow to cool.

3. While the squash is cooling, put the broccoli, spinach, and pesto in a medium bowl, stirring until well combined.

4. Once the squash is cooked and cooled slightly, using a fork, scoop out the inside of each squash half. The result will be noodle-like strands of squash. Spread the squash out in an even layer in the prepared baking dish.

5. Place the pesto vegetables in an even layer on top of the squash. Spread the cheese evenly on top.

6. Bake for 15 minutes, or until the cheese has melted. Remove from the oven and allow to cool for 2 to 4 minutes before cutting into squares and serving while still warm. Enjoy!

Something Extra: If you want to add some protein to this dish, I highly recommend a can or two of shredded chicken. For every can of shredded chicken used, add another ⅓ cup of pesto. Simply mix the shredded chicken into the pesto veggie mix.

Per serving: Calories: 321; Total Fat: 26g; Saturated Fat: 7g; Cholesterol: 27mg; Carbohydrates: 15g; Fiber: 4g; Sodium: 788mg; Protein: 11g

Garlic-Herbed Orzo and Vegetables

Prep time: 5 minutes **Cook time:** 30 minutes

Rice-like orzo pasta is tossed with sautéed vegetables, drizzled with a garlic-and-herb dressing, and finished with herb feta crumbles to add a touch of creaminess. The ingredients are easily available and result in a lip-smacking meal. It is one of my all-time favorites. **Serves 8**

5 tablespoons olive oil, divided

1¼ cups gluten-free orzo

1¾ cups vegetable broth

1 tablespoon minced garlic

½ sweet onion, diced

3 to 4 cups quartered Brussels sprouts

1 cup chopped mushrooms

1 cup diced bell pepper

½ teaspoon salt, plus more for seasoning

½ teaspoon freshly ground black pepper, plus more for seasoning

1 tablespoon freshly squeezed lemon juice

½ cup garlic-and-herb feta cheese crumbles

Almond slivers, chopped fresh basil leaves and red pepper flakes, for garnish (optional)

1. In a medium skillet, heat 1 tablespoon of oil over medium heat for 1 to 2 minutes. Stir in the orzo and cook for 2 to 3 minutes, or until golden brown. Add the broth and bring to a simmer. Cover the skillet and cook for 10 to 15 minutes, or until the orzo has soaked up the liquid. Remove from the heat.

2. While the orzo is cooking, in a large skillet, heat 2 tablespoons of oil over medium heat for 1 to 2 minutes. Stir in the garlic and onion and cook for 2 to 3 minutes, or until the onion becomes transparent and the garlic golden brown and fragrant. Add the sprouts, mushrooms, and bell pepper. Season with salt and pepper. Cook the vegetables for 8 to 10 minutes, or until they become tender and bright.

3. While the orzo and vegetables are cooking, to make the vinaigrette, whisk together the remaining 2 tablespoons of oil, the lemon juice, ½ teaspoon of salt, and ½ teaspoon of pepper. Pour the cooked orzo into the large skillet with the vegetables. Drizzle with the vinaigrette and stir to coat. Sprinkle with the cheese and stir until the cheese starts to melt and the dish becomes slightly creamy. Remove from the heat.

4. Serve warm, sprinkled with almonds, basil, and red pepper flakes (if using).

Ingredient Swap: If someone in the family is not a fan of Brussels sprouts, use chopped asparagus or broccoli spears instead.

Per serving: Calories: 205; Total Fat: 12g; Saturated Fat: 3g; Cholesterol: 10mg; Carbohydrates: 21g; Fiber: 4g; Sodium: 318mg; Protein: 6g

Veggie Egg Rolls

Prep time: 15 minutes **Cook time:** 35 minutes

If you are anything like me, egg rolls are one thing that you miss on a gluten-free diet. Those crunchy outer shells with perfectly cooked vegetables and juicy Asian-inspired sauce dripping out of every bite are too delicious not to be missed. Until now, friends. I have been trying to perfect this recipe for about a decade, and I finally have it down. Enjoy! **Makes 12 egg rolls**

FOR THE VEGETABLE STUFFING

Oil, for frying (I like to use canola oil for this recipe)
1 cup finely chopped mushrooms
1 cup shredded cabbage
1 cup shredded carrots
1 cup bean sprouts
1 can water chestnuts, drained
2 tablespoons sesame oil
2 tablespoons coconut aminos or gluten-free soy sauce
1 tablespoon rice vinegar
1½ teaspoons sugar
1 teaspoon ground ginger

TO MAKE THE VEGETABLE STUFFING

1. In a wok or nonstick skillet, heat 2 tablespoons of oil over medium heat. Add the mushrooms, cabbage, carrots, sprouts, and water chestnuts and sauté for 5 to 7 minutes, or until tender. Add the sesame oil, coconut aminos, vinegar, sugar, and ginger. Stir and cook for 3 to 4 minutes, or until the liquid has been absorbed.

2. Transfer the mixture to a bowl and place it in the refrigerator.

3. Fill the wok with at least 3 inches of oil and heat to about 350°F while you make the wrappers.

TO MAKE THE WRAPPERS

4. In a medium bowl, combine the tapioca flour, white rice flour, salt, and xanthan gum and stir well.

5. In a small bowl, mix together the eggs and water and then pour it into the flour mixture. Stir until a uniform dough forms.

FOR THE WRAPPERS

1½ cups tapioca flour

1½ cups white rice flour, plus more for dusting

1 teaspoon salt

½ teaspoon xanthan gum

2 large eggs, beaten

1 cup water, at room temperature

6. Place a large piece of parchment paper on a work surface and generously dust it with white rice flour. Generously dust a rolling pin with flour as well. Roll out the dough to a ⅛-inch thickness, dusting the rolling pin generously after every pass to help prevent sticking. Cut the dough into 6-inch squares.

7. Place equal amounts of vegetable filling in the middle of each square. Fold one corner of the wrapper over the filling, then fold the two corners that are next to the first corner across the vegetable filling. Roll the wrapper toward the first corner and press gently to seal the dough wrapper shut.

8. Line a plate with paper towels. Place 2 or 3 egg rolls at a time in the hot oil. Fry for 2 to 4 minutes, or until both sides are fried, crisp, and slightly golden brown. Use a wire strainer spoon to transfer them to the prepared plate to cool. Allow to rest for 5 minutes before serving.

Something Extra: Try dipping these egg rolls into your favorite peanut sauce, like the juicy peanut sauce from Cold Peanut Noodle Bowls (page 89).

Per serving (1 egg roll): Calories: 204; Total Fat: 8g; Saturated Fat: 1g; Cholesterol: 27mg; Carbohydrates: 30g; Fiber: 1g; Sodium: 298mg; Protein: 3g

Fajita Rice Bowls

Prep time: 15 minutes **Cook time:** 10 minutes

This recipe gives you all the flavor and texture of fajitas without the meat and tortillas. The bowls are incredibly easy to make and are perfect for meal-prepping families. After all, there's a lot to be said for a fantastically flavorful homemade meal-on-the-go that can be made with minimal effort.

Serves 4

2 tablespoons olive oil, divided
1 tablespoon minced garlic
2 bell peppers, sliced
½ sweet onion, sliced
½ teaspoon paprika
½ teaspoon chipotle chile powder (optional)
½ teaspoon ground cumin
¼ teaspoon ground coriander
1 teaspoon salt, divided
5 tablespoons chopped fresh cilantro, divided
1 cup pico de gallo
4 cups cooked white or brown rice
2 tablespoons freshly squeezed lime juice

1. In a large skillet, heat 1 tablespoon of oil over medium heat. Add the garlic and cook until it is golden and fragrant. Add the bell peppers and onion and then the paprika, chile powder, cumin, coriander, and ½ teaspoon of salt. Cook, stirring occasionally, for 4 to 6 minutes, or until the vegetables start to turn tender.

2. While the vegetables are cooking, in a small bowl, stir together 2 tablespoons of cilantro and the pico de gallo. In a large bowl, combine the cooked rice, lime juice, and remaining ½ teaspoon of salt, 1 tablespoon of oil, and 3 tablespoons of cilantro and stir well.

3. Remove the vegetables from the heat and build the rice bowls. Put one-fourth of the rice in each of 4 serving bowls. Top with one-fourth of the fajita vegetables, and lastly, one-fourth of the pico de gallo. Store leftovers in an airtight container in the refrigerator for up to 3 days.

Per serving: Calories: 335; Total Fat: 9g; Saturated Fat: 1g; Cholesterol: 0mg; Carbohydrates: 59g; Fiber: 5g; Sodium: 899mg; Protein: 6g

Lentil Taco Stuffed Peppers

Prep time: 5 minutes **Cook time:** 50 minutes

When you crave all the flavors of tacos but not the guilt or gluten, reach for this recipe. Crisp bell peppers are stuffed to the brim with fluffy quinoa and perfect lentils that have been well seasoned and stirred together with tomatoes and corn. This recipe is guaranteed to not leave leftovers.

Serves 8

5 cups water

1 cup dried lentils

1 cup quinoa

1 (15¼-ounce) can sweet corn kernels, drained

1 (14½-ounce) can diced tomatoes

2 teaspoons ground cumin

1½ teaspoons chili powder

1½ teaspoons garlic powder

1 teaspoon dried oregano

4 bell peppers, halved and seeded

1 cup shredded Cheddar cheese

1. Preheat the oven to 350°F. Line a rimmed baking sheet with aluminum foil.

2. In a large skillet, bring the water to a simmer over medium heat. Stir in the lentils and quinoa. Simmer for 15 minutes, or until the liquid is absorbed.

3. Reduce the heat to medium-low and add the corn, tomatoes, cumin, chili powder, garlic powder, and oregano. Stir to combine, then cook for 4 minutes, or until the liquid is absorbed. Remove from heat.

4. Place the bell pepper halves on the baking sheet, open-side up. Scoop the lentil and quinoa mixture into the bell pepper halves until filled to the top. Sprinkle each pepper half with 2 tablespoons of cheese and bake for 25 to 30 minutes, or until the cheese has turned into a golden brown crust and the peppers are tender and roasted.

5. Remove from the oven and allow to sit for 3 to 4 minutes to cool before serving warm.

Per serving: Calories: 285; Total Fat: 7g; Saturated Fat: 3g; Cholesterol: 14mg; Carbohydrates: 42g; Fiber: 8g; Sodium: 256mg; Protein: 15g

Stuffed Mushrooms

Prep time: 10 minutes **Cook time:** 20 minutes

Stuffed mushrooms are a great option for a quick, warm, hearty dish, with just a handful of simple ingredients melted together and stuffed inside portabella mushrooms. Stuffing the mushrooms is the fun part, and a point in the cooking process where kids can get involved and work with their hands. **Serves 8**

8 portabella mushrooms, stemmed
2 tablespoons unsalted butter
8 ounces cream cheese
4 tablespoons grated parmesan cheese, divided
2 teaspoons Italian seasoning
½ teaspoon garlic powder
¼ teaspoon freshly ground black pepper

1. Preheat the oven to 400°F. Line a rimmed baking sheet with parchment paper. Line a plate with paper towels.

2. Place the mushrooms upside down on the baking sheet, ready for stuffing.

3. In a medium skillet, combine the butter, cream cheese, 2 tablespoons of parmesan cheese, the Italian seasoning, garlic powder, and pepper. Cook over medium-low heat, stirring, for 3 to 4 minutes, or until melted and well mixed. Remove from the heat.

4. Spoon the cheese mixture evenly into each mushroom cap. Sprinkle the remaining 2 tablespoons of parmesan cheese on top.

5. Bake for 15 minutes, until the cheese is slightly golden brown. Remove from the oven. Transfer the mushrooms to the prepared plate to cool for 5 minutes before serving.

- -

Per serving: Calories: 155; Total Fat: 14g; Saturated Fat: 8g; Cholesterol: 42mg; Carbohydrates: 5g; Fiber: 1g; Sodium: 190mg; Protein: 4g

Greek-Inspired Zoodle Bowls

Prep time: 5 minutes **Cook time:** 5 minutes

If you need a simple, 10-minute recipe that will knock your socks off, this is it. Zucchini noodles, once cooked, are easy to twirl around your fork like cooked spaghetti. Kids love this dish for its spaghetti-like qualities, and adults like it for its taste and healthy ingredients. It's light, fresh, and addictive, all in one bowl, and is perfect for lunches and picnics. **Serves 4**

3 tablespoons olive oil, divided

3 medium zucchini, zoodled

2 tablespoons dried oregano

3 tablespoons red-wine vinegar

1 teaspoon freshly squeezed lemon juice

¼ teaspoon garlic powder

Salt

Freshly ground black pepper

4 medium roma tomatoes, chopped

8 ounces feta cheese crumbles

1 small red onion, diced

1. In a large nonstick skillet, heat 1 tablespoon of oil over medium heat. Add the zoodles and stir to coat. Cook, stirring occasionally, for 2 to 3 minutes, or until the zoodles become deeper in color and tender. Remove from the heat and transfer the zoodles to a large serving bowl.

2. To make the dressing, in a small bowl, combine the oregano, remaining 2 tablespoons of oil, the vinegar, lemon juice, and garlic powder. Season with salt and pepper and mix well.

3. Add the tomatoes, cheese, and onion to the zoodles. Drizzle the dressing on top and gently toss to combine and coat well. Serve immediately.

Helpful Hack: To make this recipe even quicker and easier to make, buy the already zoodled zucchini that you can find in the fresh produce section of the grocery store.

Per serving: Calories: 273; Total Fat: 20g; Saturated Fat: 10g; Cholesterol: 50mg; Carbohydrates: 15g; Fiber: 4g; Sodium: 540mg; Protein: 11g

Fresh Herb Pizza

Prep time: 20 minutes **Cook time:** 15 minutes

Our family celebrates Friday nights with homemade pizzas, and this doughy, cheesy, herby gluten-free recipe is always my go-to. From the easy-to-make, homemade thin crust to the delicious toppings, the whole family will love every single slice. Get ready for pizza nights to be the favorite night of the week. **Serves 4**

FOR THE CRUST

Gluten-free cooking spray, for coating the baking sheet

1¾ cups plus 2 tablespoons gluten-free flour blend

½ teaspoon salt

½ teaspoon xanthan gum

1 package rapid/instant yeast

½ cup plus 2 tablespoons milk

2 tablespoons unsalted butter, at room temperature

1 large egg, at room temperature

2 tablespoons honey

½ teaspoon apple cider vinegar

TO MAKE THE CRUST

1. Preheat the oven to 450°F. Spray a large nonstick baking sheet with cooking spray.

2. In a large bowl, combine the flour blend, salt, and xanthan gum. Make a small hole with your finger in the middle of the mixture and pour the yeast into that hole.

3. Warm the milk to around 115°F in the microwave, using a thermometer to check the temperature, usually 30 to 45 seconds on high power. Then pour the warm milk over the yeast in the hole.

4. Add the butter, egg, honey, and vinegar and mix using the dough hook attachment on your mixer for about 2 minutes, or until fully combined.

5. Using your hands sprayed with cooking spray, evenly place half of the dough on the prepared baking sheet and flatten it out into a large circle about 10 inches in diameter and ¼ inch thick. Shape and flatten the second half of the dough the same way on the other half of the baking sheet.

6. Bake on the middle rack for 6 to 7 minutes. Remove from the oven, leaving the oven on.

FOR THE PIZZA

½ cup spaghetti sauce

½ teaspoon garlic powder

2 cups shredded mozzarella cheese

2 tablespoons finely chopped fresh basil leaves

1 to 2 tablespoons chopped fresh rosemary leaves

TO MAKE THE PIZZA

7. Spread half of the spaghetti sauce in an even layer on the top of each pizza crust. Sprinkle half of the garlic powder evenly on each pizza crust, followed by half of the cheese, basil, and rosemary.

8. Bake on the middle rack for 5 minutes, or until the cheese is melted and the crust is golden brown. Remove from the oven. Allow to cool for 2 to 3 minutes before cutting into slices and serving.

9. Store room-temperature pizza slices in an airtight container in the refrigerator for up to 3 days.

Helpful Hack: Omit the ingredients and instructions for making the homemade pizza crust if you have a store-bought crust. If you are using homemade but previously cooked and frozen crusts, set them on a baking sheet sprayed with cooking spray before topping.

Per serving: Calories: 507; Total Fat: 21g; Saturated Fat: 12g; Cholesterol: 110mg; Carbohydrates: 64g; Fiber: 3g; Sodium: 728mg; Protein: 17g

Chicken Pot Pie,
page 113

Meat and Seafood

Fresh Fish Piccata

Prep time: 5 minutes **Cook time:** 25 minutes

Breaded fish is always popular, and when it is mixed with al dente pasta and smothered in a zesty sauce, it's even better. The cream-based sauce thickens as it cooks, and the delicate capers pack a punch of flavor and give the dish its final touch. **Serves 4**

5 tablespoons unsalted butter

2 tablespoons white rice flour

¼ cup grated parmesan cheese, divided

½ teaspoon garlic powder

½ teaspoon salt

4 thin fish fillets (cod or tilapia are great choices)

2 tablespoons minced garlic

1¾ cups chicken broth or stock

1¼ cups heavy cream

3 tablespoons capers

3 tablespoons freshly squeezed lemon juice

8 ounces spaghetti or linguine, broken in half

1. In a large nonstick skillet, melt the butter over medium heat. While the butter is melting, stir together the flour, ¼ cup of parmesan cheese, the garlic powder, and salt on a large plate until well mixed.

2. Lightly coat each fish fillet in the flour mixture, then place 2 to 4 fish fillets (depending on the size of the skillet and the fillets, you may need to cook in 2 batches) in the skillet and cook for 2 to 4 minutes on the first side, or until there is a nice golden brown crust. Then carefully flip each fillet and cook for another 2 to 4 minutes, or until the internal temperature reaches 165°F. Transfer the fish fillets to a plate and keep warm.

3. Add the garlic to the skillet and sauté for 1 to 2 minutes, or until fragrant and starting to turn golden brown. Then add the broth, cream, capers, and lemon juice, giving it all a good stir. Add the spaghetti, covering it with sauce to ensure that it is cooked evenly.

4. Cook the spaghetti according to the package directions, but take it off the heat 1 or 2 minutes early, depending on how al dente or tender you like the noodles. Stir occasionally throughout the cooking process.

5. Remove from the heat. Give the spaghetti and sauce a quick stir and plate it. Place the fish on top of the pasta. Drizzle a spoonful of extra sauce on top of the fish and enjoy while hot.

Ingredient Swap: If you prefer chicken over fish, substitute thin chicken breasts for the fish for a beautiful chicken piccata meal.

Per serving: Calories: 810; Total Fat: 51g; Saturated Fat: 30g; Cholesterol: 202mg; Carbohydrates: 59g; Fiber: 7g; Sodium: 1,120mg; Protein: 32g

Country-Fried Steak with Gravy

Prep time: 5 minutes **Cook time:** 35 minutes

This stick-to-your-ribs version of country-fried steak uses the perfect blend of spices for the breading and creates a deliciously smooth and thick country gravy, without a lick of gluten. **Serves 4**

FOR THE STEAKS

Oil, for frying
3 large eggs
1½ cups gluten-free flour blend
1½ teaspoons garlic salt
½ teaspoon onion powder
1½ teaspoons paprika
1 teaspoon freshly ground black pepper
4 thin-cut steaks or cubed steak patties

FOR THE GRAVY

2 tablespoons unsalted butter
¼ cup gluten-free flour blend
1¾ cups chicken broth
½ cup heavy cream
¼ teaspoon salt
½ teaspoon freshly ground black pepper

TO MAKE THE STEAKS

1. Preheat the oven to 325°F. Set a cooling rack over paper towels or a plate.

2. Pour ½ inch of oil into a skillet over medium heat.

3. In a medium bowl, beat the eggs. In another medium bowl, stir together the flour blend, garlic salt, onion powder, paprika, and pepper.

4. Coat all sides of 1 piece of steak in the flour. Then dredge in the egg bath, submerging all sides and allowing the excess to fall off the meat before placing the steak back into the flour mixture, coating all sides once more.

5. Immediately place the steak in the hot skillet and cook for 4 minutes. Repeat the coating process with the remaining 3 steaks and add them to the skillet.

6. After each steak has cooked for 4 minutes, carefully flip them and cook for another 4 to 5 minutes, or until cooked thoroughly.

7. Remove them from the hot oil using a spatula and place the steaks on the cooling rack. Keep warm.

8. In a medium saucepan, melt the butter over medium heat. Add the flour blend and continuously mix for 30 seconds, or until the liquid is fully absorbed. Add the broth ⅓ cup at a time, waiting until the gravy returns to a simmer before stirring and adding the next ⅓ cup. Do the same with the cream. Add the salt and pepper and simmer for 5 to 10 minutes. Remove from the heat.

9. Serve the fried steaks with the gravy drizzled on top. Store any leftovers in an airtight container in the refrigerator for up to 3 days, keeping the steaks and the gravy separate when storing.

Prep Tip: I highly recommend Bob's Red Mill 1:1 Gluten-Free Baking Flour for this recipe since it is easily accessible for most home cooks and is a more affordable option, too.

Per serving: Calories: 512; Total Fat: 29g; Saturated Fat: 13g; Cholesterol: 202mg; Carbohydrates: 36g; Fiber: 1g; Sodium: 438mg; Protein: 27g

Pork Chops with Creamy Gravy

Prep time: 5 minutes **Cook time:** 25 minutes

This one-pot recipe uses either bone-in or boneless pork chops to create a juicy meal simmering in thick and creamy gravy. It's perfectly paired with your favorite steamed vegetables, especially if you add an additional dollop of that dreamy gravy right on top. This recipe is a quick and easy meal ready in 30 minutes, but it tastes like you've been working away in the kitchen all day. **Serves 4**

2 tablespoons unsalted butter
½ medium sweet onion, chopped
4 pork chops
1 teaspoon garlic powder
Salt
Freshly ground black pepper
1 cup chicken stock
1 tablespoon gluten-free Worcestershire sauce
1½ tablespoons cornstarch
⅓ cup sliced mushroom pieces
½ cup sour cream

1. Heat a large nonstick skillet over medium heat. Add the butter and onion and cook, stirring occasionally, for 2 to 3 minutes, or until the onion is softened.

2. Sprinkle the pork chops with the garlic powder, season with salt and pepper, then add them to the skillet and sear on each side for 2 to 3 minutes, until both sides are lightly browned.

3. Add the stock and Worcestershire sauce, scraping the browned bits from the bottom of the skillet (they carry so much flavor). Continue cooking the pork chops, flipping every 2 to 3 minutes, for 4 to 6 minutes, or until the internal temperature reaches 145°F. (Note: Bone-in pork chops and pork chops thicker than ¾ inch will likely need an additional 1 to 3 minutes of cook time.)

4.   Transfer the chops (keep liquids in the skillet) to a separate plate and put it in the microwave to keep warm, covered. Add the cornstarch, mushrooms, and sour cream to the hot skillet, stir to combine, and simmer the gravy for 3 to 4 minutes, or until slightly thickened. Return the pork chops to the skillet, remove from the heat, and serve.

Helpful Hack: If you don't like mushrooms in the gravy, leave them out and plan on thickening the gravy for only 2 to 3 minutes.

Per serving: Calories: 353; Total Fat: 22g; Saturated Fat: 10g; Cholesterol: 110mg; Carbohydrates: 10g; Fiber: 1g; Sodium: 292mg; Protein: 26g

Sweet and Sour Chicken

Prep time: 5 minutes **Cook time:** 55 minutes

If you've got a craving for Chinese takeout, this recipe is sure to satisfy. The gluten-free coating on the tender chicken bakes the pieces to golden perfection. This dish is amazing served with a side of Flash-Fried Green Beans (page 69) or Veggie Fried Rice (page 83). **Serves 4**

⅓ cup coconut oil

2 large eggs

1½ cups cornstarch

1½ tablespoons garlic powder, divided

¼ teaspoon salt

¼ teaspoon freshly ground black pepper

1½ cups brown or white rice flour

1½ pounds chicken breast meat, cubed

7 tablespoons gluten-free sweet chili paste

1 cup sugar

⅓ cup apple cider vinegar

3 tablespoons gluten-free soy sauce

1. Preheat the oven to 350°F. Pour the coconut oil into a 9-by-13-inch baking dish and evenly distribute the oil over the bottom.

2. In a medium bowl, beat the eggs.

3. In a large resealable plastic bag, combine the cornstarch, 1 tablespoon of garlic powder, the salt, and pepper and mix well. Pour the flour into a separate large resealable plastic bag.

4. Dip the chicken pieces into the eggs and allow the excess to drip off. Then drop the chicken pieces into the bag with the flour, zip the bag up tightly, and shake the contents until evenly coated. Transfer the pieces to the bag with the cornstarch mixture and do the same shaking technique.

5. Put the coated chicken pieces in the prepared baking dish and bake for 45 minutes, stirring every 15 minutes to allow the chicken to cook and crisp evenly.

6. While the chicken is baking, to make the sauce, in a medium bowl, combine the chili sauce, sugar, vinegar, soy sauce, and remaining ½ tablespoon of garlic powder.

7. Once the 45 minutes are up, pour the sauce on the chicken and stir to make sure that all pieces are entirely covered.

8. Bake for another 10 minutes, or until the chicken is fully cooked and the sauce starts to thicken and turn into a glaze.

9. Remove from the oven and serve while still warm. The sauce will thicken slightly as it cools.

10. Store room-temperature leftovers in an airtight container in the refrigerator for up to 3 days. Reheat in the microwave in a microwave-safe dish on high power for 45 to 60 seconds, or until the desired temperature is reached.

Ingredient Swap: You can substitute the following ingredients in a 1:1 ratio: liquid or coconut aminos for the gluten-free soy sauce, coconut sugar for the granulated sugar, and arrowroot starch for the cornstarch.

Per serving: Calories: 756; Total Fat: 24g; Saturated Fat: 17g; Cholesterol: 190mg; Carbohydrates: 89g; Fiber: 3g; Sodium: 957mg; Protein: 45g

Chicken Marsala

Prep time: 5 minutes **Cook time:** 1 hour

Chicken Marsala is an Italian-inspired dish that effortlessly blends juicy chicken and a red wine and mushroom sauce. The aroma from the garlic and thyme will permeate the whole house in a dreamy dinnertime delight. See the tip for a slow cooker version in case busy weeknight dinners need a little help. **Serves 4**

2 tablespoons unsalted
  butter or olive oil
2 tablespoons minced garlic
4 boneless, skinless chicken
  breasts, seasoned with salt
  and pepper
1 to 2 cups sliced
  mushrooms
1 cup Marsala wine
1 cup cherry tomatoes,
  halved
2 to 3 tablespoons chopped
  fresh thyme leaves
½ cup water
¼ cup cornstarch
Fresh parsley, for garnish

1. Put the butter, garlic, and chicken in a large Dutch oven over medium heat. Sear the chicken on each side for 5 to 7 minutes.

2. Stir in the mushrooms, wine, tomatoes, and thyme and bring to a simmer. Cover and slowly simmer for 45 to 50 minutes, or until the chicken is fully cooked.

3. Halfway through cooking, in a small bowl, whisk together the water and cornstarch until fully dissolved. Pour the liquid into the Dutch oven, stir well, and continue to simmer. Sprinkle with parsley, remove from the heat, and serve warm.

- -

Helpful Hack: Try the slow cooker version of this recipe. Put all the ingredients in the slow cooker and cook on low for 6 hours or on high for 3 to 4 hours.

- -

Per serving: Calories: 334; Total Fat: 9g; Saturated Fat: 4g; Cholesterol: 98mg; Carbohydrates: 20g; Fiber: 1g; Sodium: 62mg; Protein: 27g

Chicken Pot Pie

Prep time: 5 minutes **Cook time:** 40 minutes

Each hearty layer of this gluten-free chicken pot pie is packed with savory flavor. You will not be able to resist the fluffy, buttery crust on top. This incredible dish is easy to adapt for those who would like a nut-free or dairy-free version (or both), so everyone will be happy. **Serves 6 to 8**

9 tablespoons unsalted butter, melted, divided

3½ cups shredded cooked chicken

1 teaspoon minced garlic

1½ cups gluten-free Bisquick mix or Homemade Gluten-Free Baking Mix, (page 13)

1 large egg, beaten

1⅔ cups heavy cream, divided

2½ cups chicken broth

1 teaspoon garlic salt

½ teaspoon freshly ground black pepper

1½ cups frozen vege-table mix

⅓ cup white rice flour

½ teaspoon xanthan gum

1. Preheat the oven to 375°F.

2. Pour 5 tablespoons of melted butter into a large oven-safe skillet or Dutch oven. Add the chicken and garlic and cook over medium heat for about 2 minutes, or until the garlic is fragrant.

3. In a large bowl, combine the baking mix, egg, remaining 4 tablespoons of melted butter, and ⅔ cup of cream and stir well.

4. Add the broth, garlic salt, and pepper to the chicken in the skillet and bring to a simmer (typically takes 4 to 5 minutes). Add the remaining 1 cup of cream and the vegetables. Once simmering, whisk in the flour and xanthan gum and cook for 2 minutes.

5. Flatten balls of biscuit dough with your hands until about ¼ inch thick. Evenly place the dough pieces on top of the chicken. Bake for 25 minutes, then broil for 2 minutes if you want a golden brown top.

6. Remove from the oven. Allow to cool and set for 5 minutes before serving.

Per serving: Calories: 1,055; Total Fat: 71g; Saturated Fat: 41g; Cholesterol: 348mg; Carbohydrates: 57g; Fiber: 3g; Sodium: 840mg; Protein: 46g

Chicken Nuggets

Prep time: 10 minutes **Cook time:** 20 minutes

Almond-crusted chicken tenders make for an incredible low-carb, protein-packed dish that's slightly sweet and oh so savory. Everyone will love it, guaranteed. These nuggets are great as an appetizer or as a main meal—the choice is yours. **Serves 4**

Gluten-free cooking spray, for coating the baking sheet

1 large egg

¼ cup gluten-free all-purpose flour

4 tablespoons (½ stick) unsalted butter or olive oil

1 tablespoon garlic powder

1½ teaspoons minced garlic

1 teaspoon freshly ground black pepper

1 teaspoon paprika

¼ teaspoon ground cumin

1 cup almonds, ground in a food processor

2 large boneless, skinless chicken breasts, cut into nuggets

1. Preheat the oven to 400°F. Line a baking sheet with aluminum foil. Lightly spray the foil with cooking spray.

2. In a small bowl, beat the egg. Pour the flour into a separate large bowl.

3. In a medium skillet, melt the butter over medium-low heat. Add the garlic powder, garlic, pepper, paprika, and cumin and mix well. Add the almonds and brown for about 5 minutes. Remove from the heat. Allow the breading mixture to cool for a few minutes before transferring it to a small bowl (so you don't burn your hands while breading the chicken).

4. Dip each chicken nugget into the flour, making sure to get all sides coated. Then dip into the egg, wipe off any excess egg, and dip into the almond mixture, pressing it onto each chicken nugget with your fingers.

5. Put each nugget on the baking sheet and bake for 14 to 16 minutes, or until the nuggets are golden brown and cooked thoroughly. Remove from the oven.

Something Extra: Add ¼ teaspoon cayenne pepper for a spicy version of these chicken nuggets. Then dip them into homemade Honey-Mustard Dressing (page 164), like my family likes to do. Voilà: a little sweet and a little spicy and a lot good.

Per serving: Calories: 384; Total Fat: 26g; Saturated Fat: 9g; Cholesterol: 129mg; Carbohydrates: 14g; Fiber: 4g; Sodium: 144mg; Protein: 24g

Spaghetti and Meatballs

Prep time: 25 minutes **Cook time:** 20 minutes

Everyone knows that Momma's spaghetti and meatballs can't be beat. This gluten-free version uses Momma's spaghetti sauce and combines it with hand-rolled meatballs that are so soft and juicy, you won't even realize that they are gluten-free. Place both of these comfort food staples on top of tender gluten-free pasta, and you have a reason to celebrate. **Serves 4 to 6**

FOR THE MEATBALLS

1 pound ground beef

1 large egg, beaten

1 tablespoon finely chopped onion

½ teaspoon minced garlic

1¼ teaspoons liquid aminos, coconut aminos, or gluten-free soy sauce

¼ teaspoon salt

¼ teaspoon freshly ground black pepper

TO MAKE THE MEATBALLS

1. Preheat the oven to 400°F. Line a plate with paper towels.

2. In a large bowl, combine the ground beef, egg, onion, garlic, liquid aminos, salt, and pepper and thoroughly mix together with your hands.

3. Roll the mixture into 1- to 1½-inch balls and put them in the cups of a mini muffin tin.

4. Bake for 10 minutes, remove them from the oven, flip them using tongs, and bake for an additional 5 minutes, or until thoroughly cooked and the outsides are nicely browned. Remove from the oven.

5. Carefully transfer the hot meatballs to the prepared plate to help soak up any extra grease.

TO MAKE THE SAUCE AND ASSEMBLE

6. While the meatballs are baking, in a saucepan or Dutch oven, combine the tomato paste, bay leaves, sugar, garlic salt, oregano, water, garlic, cheese, pepper, and onion flakes over medium heat. Stir well.

2 (6-ounce) cans tomato paste

3 bay leaves

2 teaspoons sugar

½ teaspoon garlic salt

3 tablespoons dried oregano

3 cups water

1 teaspoon minced garlic

3 tablespoons grated parmesan cheese

½ teaspoon freshly ground black pepper

1½ tablespoons dried onion flakes

1 (16-ounce) package gluten-free pasta

7. Simmer for 20 minutes. Remove from the heat. Allow to cool for 2 to 3 minutes before serving.

8. While the sauce is simmering, cook the pasta according to the package instructions so that the pasta is done at the same time as the sauce (time varies widely depending on the brand and type of pasta). Drain the pasta.

9. Serve the pasta warm, topped with meatballs and drizzled with spaghetti sauce. Store cooled meatballs in an airtight container in the refrigerator for up to 3 days.

Helpful Hack: Use an ice cream scoop to easily scoop out the ground beef mixture into round, perfectly sized meatballs.

Per serving: Calories: 478; Total Fat: 10g; Saturated Fat: 4g; Cholesterol: 120mg; Carbohydrates: 67g; Fiber: 11g; Sodium: 409mg; Protein: 35g

Chicken Salad

Prep time: 5 minutes

In this take on the classic chicken salad, I use Greek yogurt as the creamy base for a healthier option and to give the dish a lighter note. When combined with the herbs, lemon juice, nuts, and dried berries, it makes for a tangy and sweet meal that gets more addictive by the bite. Try serving this over a bed of fresh lettuce or in between your favorite gluten-free sandwich bread. **Serves 4**

4 cups shredded
   cooked chicken
1 apple, chopped
⅓ cup dried cranberries
⅓ cup finely chopped celery
¼ red onion, chopped
¼ cup chopped pecans
½ cup plain nonfat
   Greek yogurt
2 tablespoons chopped
   fresh rosemary leaves, plus
   more for garnish
1 tablespoon red-wine
   vinegar
2 tablespoons honey
½ tablespoon freshly
   squeezed lemon juice
Freshly ground black pepper

1. In a large bowl, combine the chicken, apple, cranberries, celery, onion, and pecans.

2. In a medium bowl, mix together the yogurt, rosemary, vinegar, honey, and lemon juice. Season with pepper. Combine with the chicken until evenly coated.

3. Store in an airtight container in the refrigerator for 2 to 3 days.

Prep Tip: Gala or Honeycrisp apples provide the correct balance of sweet and zesty.

Per serving: Calories: 371; Total Fat: 11g; Saturated Fat: 2g; Cholesterol: 106mg; Carbohydrates: 26g; Fiber: 3g; Sodium: 90mg; Protein: 42g

5 INGREDIENT, 30 MINUTES OR LESS, DAIRY-FREE, LOW-CARB

Blackened Fish Fillets

Prep time: 5 minutes **Cook time:** 10 minutes

This blackened fish recipe uses three simple ingredients and creates blackened flounder fillets that are savory and crisp on the outside and full of spices and perfectly light and flaky on the inside. Create a fabulous fish dinner tonight in less than half an hour. **Serves 4**

6 tablespoons blacken-
   ing spice
4 (6-ounce) flounder fillets
2 tablespoons coconut oil

1. Heat the broiler to high. Line a plate with paper towels.

2. Spread the spice on a plate and coat each fillet on both sides until fully covered with spice.

3. In a large oven-safe sauté pan, heat the oil over medium-high heat. Put the fillets in the pan and cook for 1 to 2 minutes, occasionally basting with a bit of the hot oil. Brush the oil on lightly so that the blackening spice does not come off on the brush.

4. Place the pan under the broiler and broil for 5 to 7 minutes, or until the internal temperature of the fillets reaches 145°F.

5. Remove from the oven (carefully; the pan handle will be hot), transfer the fillets to the prepared plate for 1 to 2 minutes, then serve while still warm.

Per serving: Calories: 199; Total Fat: 11g; Saturated Fat: 7g; Cholesterol: 79mg; Carbohydrates: 4g; Fiber: 2g; Sodium: 811mg; Protein: 22g

Beef Stir-Fry

Prep time: 5 minutes **Cook time:** 20 minutes

Beef stir-fry is one of my family's favorite weeknight meals. This recipe incorporates an affordable piece of beef and other simple ingredients, resulting in juicy beef pieces and tender vegetables. It's one of the easiest ways to get kids to eat their veggies. **Serves 4**

1½ pounds sliced stir-fry beef

½ cup sliced carrots

½ tablespoon minced garlic

2 tablespoons sesame oil, divided

Pinch freshly ground black pepper

1 cup chopped broccoli florets

2 tablespoons coconut sugar or packed light brown sugar

2 tablespoons liquid aminos or gluten-free soy sauce

1½ tablespoons honey

1 tablespoon rice vinegar

½ teaspoon freshly squeezed lime juice

⅛ teaspoon ground ginger

1 medium zucchini, sliced

1½ cups green beans

½ medium onion, sliced

1. In a large skillet, combine the beef, carrots, garlic, 1 tablespoon of oil, and the pepper.

2. Stir-fry over medium heat for 8 to 12 minutes, or until the beef is fully cooked and the carrot slices are starting to soften.

3. While the beef is cooking, in a small bowl, mix together the sugar, liquid aminos, honey, vinegar, the remaining 1 tablespoon of oil, the lime juice, and ginger.

4. Add the zucchini, green beans, onion, and broccoli to the skillet. Drizzle the sauce over the beef and vegetables and continue to cook for about 5 minutes, or until the vegetables become slightly tender and begin to soak up the sauce. Remove from the heat.

Ingredient Swap: You can easily swap out the beef for chicken. Simply use 1 to 1½ pounds cubed chicken breast. You may need to cook the chicken pieces for 1 to 3 minutes longer than you would the beef.

Per serving: Calories: 372; Total Fat: 16g; Saturated Fat: 4g; Cholesterol: 112mg; Carbohydrates: 20g; Fiber: 3g; Sodium: 419mg; Protein: 40g

Roasted Honey-Garlic Pork and Vegetables

Prep time: 5 minutes **Cook time:** 30 minutes

This is a quick and easy weeknight meal prepared in a little more than 30 minutes. This recipe has all the perks of a one-pot dish in that it mixes tender meat and roasted vegetables together so the flavors meld, and there are only two dishes to clean afterward. **Serves 4**

Gluten-free cooking spray, for coating the baking dish
1 pound pork tenderloin, cut into 1-inch-thick slices
1 (14-ounce) can sweet corn kernels, drained
1 large zucchini, sliced
1 cup cubed butternut squash
½ cup honey
2 tablespoons gluten-free soy sauce or liquid aminos
2 tablespoons freshly squeezed lime juice
2 tablespoons minced garlic
2 tablespoons olive oil
1 teaspoon fresh thyme leaves
¼ teaspoon paprika
Salt
Freshly ground black pepper
2 tablespoons sunflower seeds (optional)

1. Preheat the oven to 425°F. Spray a 9-by-13-inch baking dish with cooking spray.

2. Spread the pork, corn, zucchini, and squash out in the prepared baking dish.

3. To make the sauce, in a medium bowl, combine the honey, soy sauce, lime juice, garlic, oil, thyme, and paprika. Season with salt and pepper and mix well. Drizzle the sauce over the vegetables and meat and roast for 20 minutes.

4. Sprinkle the sunflower seeds (if using) on top of the dish and roast for another 5 to 10 minutes, or until the internal temperature of the pork has reached 150°F. Remove from the oven and allow to cool for 5 minutes before serving.

Ingredient Swap: If you don't have sunflower seeds on hand but you have pecans, peanuts, or walnuts, use those as a beautifully crunchy alternative.

Per serving: Calories: 422; Total Fat: 12g; Saturated Fat: 2g; Cholesterol: 74mg; Carbohydrates: 55g; Fiber: 4g; Sodium: 469mg; Protein: 28g

ONE POT, 30 MINUTES OR LESS, DAIRY-FREE, LOW-CARB

Thai-Inspired Turkey Lettuce Wraps

Prep time: 5 minutes **Cook time:** 15 minutes

Speedy, flavorful, crunchy, and low carb, these turkey lettuce wraps make for a great lunch. Let the fixings fall and scoop up the extras for even more delicious lettuce wraps. **Serves 4**

2 tablespoons sesame oil or olive oil

2 teaspoons minced garlic

2 scallions, both green and white parts, chopped

1 pound ground turkey

⅓ cup mushrooms (optional)

6 tablespoons sweet chili paste

1½ tablespoons gluten-free soy sauce or coconut aminos

1 handful fresh basil leaves, chopped

1 head iceberg lettuce, for wraps

1. Heat a wok over medium-high heat for 2 to 3 minutes. Pour in the oil, then add the garlic and scallions and stir-fry for 1 to 2 minutes, or until aromatic.

2. Add the turkey and mushrooms (if using). Cook, using a spatula to stir-fry and break the meat into small lumps, for 5 to 7 minutes, or until the turkey is browned and fully cooked.

3. Toss in the chili paste and soy sauce and combine well.

4. Add the basil and do a few quick stirs until the basil leaves start to become wilted and fragrant. Remove from the heat. Serve immediately in lettuce leaf wraps.

- -

Something Extra: If you like spice, try adding 1 diced seeded jalapeño when you cook the turkey and mushrooms. You can also sprinkle the top of each lettuce wrap with a pinch of red pepper flakes.

- -

Per serving: Calories: 289; Total Fat: 16g; Saturated Fat: 3g; Cholesterol: 78mg; Carbohydrates: 12g; Fiber: 4g; Sodium: 620mg; Protein: 25g

ONE POT, NUT-FREE

White Wine Cream–Dipped Pork Medallions

Prep time: 5 minutes **Cook time:** 40 minutes

If any pork dish is going to taste over-the-top gourmet, this is it. The combination of cream, white wine, and fresh herbs make this dish taste incredibly sophisticated without you having to use any fancy techniques or one-of-a-kind expensive ingredients. With the flavors of this dish, you won't need to worry about leftovers. **Serves 4**

4 tablespoons (½ stick) unsalted butter
1 pork tenderloin, cut into 1½-inch medallion slices
½ medium red onion, chopped
1½ tablespoons minced garlic
1 cup chopped mushrooms
½ cup bacon bits
¾ cup dry white wine
1 cup cream
3 tablespoons chopped fresh rosemary or thyme leaves
Salt
Freshly ground black pepper

1. In a large skillet, melt the butter over medium heat. Add the pork and brown on each side for 5 minutes, then transfer to a plate to rest.

2. Add the onion and garlic to the skillet and sauté for 3 to 4 minutes, or until the onion becomes translucent and fragrant. Then add the mushrooms and bacon and sauté for 3 to 4 minutes, or until the mushrooms are tender.

3. Return the pork to the skillet and add the wine. Cover and simmer for 5 minutes. Remove the cover and add the cream and rosemary. Season with salt and pepper and bring to a simmer. Cook, stirring occasionally, for 10 to 13 minutes, or until the sauce has reduced to one-fourth of its original amount and the internal temperature of the pork reaches 145°F. Serve.

Per serving: Calories: 549; Total Fat: 41g; Saturated Fat: 24g; Cholesterol: 197mg; Carbohydrates: 6g; Fiber: 1g; Sodium: 371mg; Protein: 30g

Fish and Chips

Prep time: 10 minutes **Cook time:** 40 minutes

Fish and chips: an all-in-one meal that is just so comforting and irresistible. This version uses an easy gluten-free batter for the fish that quickly fries in a small amount of oil before the fish gets transferred to the oven to finish cooking. I like this two-step process much better than deep-frying because it is healthier and less messy. Plus, the chips will be in the oven baking already, so it just makes sense to let those fish pieces join them for the last few minutes of dinner prep. **Serves 2 to 4**

FOR THE FISH

Oil, for frying
⅓ cup white rice flour
½ teaspoon xanthan gum
2 large eggs, beaten
½ teaspoon baking powder
1 teaspoon salt, divided
¼ teaspoon cayenne pepper
½ cup heavy cream
1 pound fresh cod fillets, cut into strips
½ teaspoon freshly ground black pepper

FOR THE CHIPS

2 large Russet potatoes, cut into ½- to ¼-inch slices or "coins"
1 tablespoon olive oil
¼ teaspoon garlic salt

TO MAKE THE FISH

1. In a large skillet, heat ½ inch of oil over medium heat for 2 to 3 minutes. Preheat the oven to 375°F and place an oven-safe wire rack on a rimmed baking sheet.

2. In a medium bowl, combine the flour and xanthan gum and mix well. Add the eggs, baking powder, ½ teaspoon of salt, and the cayenne and mix well. Add the cream and mix until a smooth batter forms.

3. Sprinkle both sides of each cod strip evenly with the remaining ½ teaspoon of salt and the black pepper. Dip each cod strip into the batter and coat evenly with a thin layer.

4. Immediately place each battered cod strip into the hot oil, leaving about 1 inch of space between them (you may need to work in batches). Fry the cod strips for 2 to 3 minutes, or until the batter is turning a nice golden brown, then, using a spatula or silicone tongs, carefully flip each cod strip and fry until golden on the second side. Remove from the heat.

5. Carefully transfer each cod strip to the wire rack. Bake for 5 to 10 minutes, checking after 5 minutes, or until the cod flakes easily under pressure. Remove from the oven to cool.

TO MAKE THE CHIPS

6. Line a baking sheet with parchment paper.

7. In a bowl, combine the potatoes, oil, and garlic salt and mix well. Spread the potatoes out evenly on the prepared baking sheet. Bake for 40 minutes, flipping once halfway through baking.

8. The fish and chips should be done at about the same time, so serve them both while still warm. Store room-temperature leftovers in an airtight container in the refrigerator for up to 2 days.

Helpful Hack: The best way to reheat leftover fish and chips is in a preheated 325°F oven. Put the fish and chips on a baking sheet and bake for 5 to 7 minutes, or until the inside of the fish is quite warm to the touch.

Per serving: Calories: 503; Total Fat: 24g; Saturated Fat: 9g; Cholesterol: 187mg; Carbohydrates: 45g; Fiber: 3g; Sodium: 882mg; Protein: 26g

Ground Beef Flautas

Prep time: 5 minutes **Cook time:** 25 minutes

Flautas are spiced ground or shredded meat rolled inside tortillas and fried for an extra crunch. This version takes flautas to the next level by briefly simmering them in a small bit of oil and then finishing them in the oven with warm, gooey cheese and pico de gallo. Prepared this way, they are much less greasy but still have the texture and flavor of a deep-fried flauta. For an added kick, drizzle a little Enchilada Sauce (page 162) between the flautas and the cheese before placing them in the oven. **Serves 4**

Oil, for frying (corn oil or canola oil work great)

1 pound ground beef

1 tablespoon chili powder

1 teaspoon ground cumin

1 teaspoon garlic powder

1 teaspoon paprika

½ tablespoon onion powder

½ teaspoon dried oregano

¼ teaspoon cayenne pepper (optional)

¼ teaspoon salt

¼ teaspoon red pepper flakes (optional)

¼ teaspoon freshly ground black pepper

1 package gluten-free tortillas

2 cups shredded cheese (Colby Jack or Monterey Jack are great choices)

1 cup pico de gallo

1. Preheat the oven to 375°F.

2. Pour 1 tablespoon of oil into a large oven-safe skillet over medium heat. Add the ground beef and cook for 3 to 5 minutes, or until fully cooked. Add the chili powder, cumin, garlic powder, paprika, onion powder, oregano, cayenne (if using), salt, red pepper flakes (if using), and black pepper, stir well, and cook for an additional 1 minute.

3. Use a slotted spoon to transfer the spiced beef to a plate, leaving any excess grease in the skillet. Add just enough oil to the hot skillet to cover the bottom (this will depend on how much fat cooked off the beef and the size of the skillet), usually 2 to 5 tablespoons.

4. Increase the heat to medium-high. Place enough beef on each tortilla so that the tortilla can still wrap around itself one full time. Wrap up the tortillas and place them, seam-side down, in the hot skillet. You may have to work in batches.

5. Fry for 2 to 3 minutes, or until the tortillas start to turn golden brown. Then flip and fry the other side for another 2 to 3 minutes, or until browned.

6. Sprinkle the cheese in an even layer on top, followed by the pico de gallo. Bake for 5 to 7 minutes, or until the cheese has melted. Remove from the oven. Allow to cool for 3 to 5 minutes before serving.

Helpful Hack: Use a large flat spatula and tongs to gently flip each flauta in the skillet without opening up the tortilla or spilling the beef.

Per serving: Calories: 589; Total Fat: 32g; Saturated Fat: 14g; Cholesterol: 128mg; Carbohydrates: 34g; Fiber: 2g; Sodium: 1,102mg; Protein: 42g

Chicken Alfredo

Prep time: 5 minutes **Cook time:** 25 minutes

Chicken alfredo is one of those dishes that every child and adult loves. There is something about the creamy garlicky sauce smothering perfectly tender noodles and juicy bites of chicken that just gets everyone on board. Take a look at the tip for how to make sure the pasta stays fresh and al dente for the family to enjoy. **Serves 6 to 8**

3 medium chicken breasts, cubed

1 tablespoon unsalted butter

2 tablespoons minced garlic

¼ cup white or brown rice flour

3 cups milk or cream

10 ounces gluten-free penne pasta

1½ teaspoons onion powder

1 cup chopped broccoli

⅓ cup freshly grated parmesan cheese

1. Heat a large skillet over medium heat for 1 to 2 minutes. Add the chicken and cook for about 10 minutes, or until browned on all sides and the internal temperature is 165°F. Transfer the chicken to a plate inside the microwave to stay warm.

2. Add the butter and garlic to the skillet. Once the butter is melted, add the flour and stir for 20 to 30 seconds, or until the flour absorbs all the liquid. Then add the milk ½ cup at a time, stirring occasionally. Once the first ½ cup of milk starts to simmer, you can add the next ½ cup and so on, until all the milk has been added.

3. Cook the pasta according to the package instructions, usually about 10 minutes, so that the pasta is likely done at the same time as the sauce.

4. Once all the milk has been added to the skillet, stir in the onion powder and simmer for 5 to 10 minutes, or until the sauce starts to thicken. Stir in the broccoli and cheese and simmer for another 1 to 2 minutes before adding the chicken and pasta to the skillet with the sauce.

5. Remove from the heat, stir to toss and coat, and serve while warm and steamy.

Cooking Tip: Gluten-free pasta can be tricky; you can end up with a grainy, mushy mess if you aren't careful. To ensure that the pasta comes out perfectly al dente, cook it for 2 minutes less than the instructions call for. Don't worry, the pasta will finish cooking in the skillet with the sauce and chicken.

Per serving: Calories: 380; Total Fat: 10g; Saturated Fat: 5g; Cholesterol: 53mg; Carbohydrates: 52g; Fiber: 6g; Sodium: 203mg; Protein: 23g

Basil Butter Steak

Prep time: 5 minutes **Cook time:** 10 minutes

This perfect date-night recipe is ready in under 20 minutes and uses just a handful of simple ingredients. Partner these steaks with some hearty Au Gratin Potatoes (page 76), Flash-Fried Green Beans (page 69), and a bottle of smooth red wine, and you will have no reason to leave the house for date night ever again. **Serves 2 to 4**

7 tablespoons unsalted butter, at room temperature, divided

4 small or 2 large (halved) 1½-inch-thick rib eye steaks, salted 2 to 24 hours before cooking

Salt

Freshly ground black pepper

4 teaspoons fresh chopped basil leaves

1 teaspoon fresh chopped thyme leaves

½ teaspoon garlic powder

1. Preheat the broiler to low. In a large oven-safe skillet, melt 3 tablespoons of butter over medium to medium-high heat. While the butter is melting, pat dry the steaks and season with salt and pepper.

2. Sear the steaks in the skillet for 1 to 2 minutes, or until a dark sear forms. Using tongs, flip the steaks over and sear for 1 to 2 minutes to create a dark sear on the second side.

3. Put the skillet in the hot oven and broil for 2 to 3 minutes before flipping and broiling for an additional 2 to 3 minutes for a medium-rare steak.

4. Remove from the oven and let sit for 5 minutes to allow the juices to redistribute.

5. While the steak is resting, in a small bowl, combine the remaining 4 tablespoons of butter, the basil, thyme, and garlic powder and mix thoroughly. Top each steak with equal amounts of butter, which will softly melt into the steak.

Per serving: Calories: 593; Total Fat: 44g; Saturated Fat: 22g; Cholesterol: 204mg; Carbohydrates: 4g; Fiber: 1g; Sodium: 665mg; Protein: 46g

Zucchini Lasagna

Prep time: 15 minutes **Cook time:** 1 hour

If all the warm, cheesy tastes of lasagna without the carbs sounds delicious, then this zucchini version is the perfect dish for you. You won't be missing a thing when you bite into hot, garlicky, cheesy layer upon layer of hearty goodness. **Serves 4**

Gluten-free cooking spray, for coating the baking dish
2 tablespoons minced garlic
½ cup diced onion
1 tablespoon olive oil
1 pound ground beef or ground turkey
2 large zucchini, cut lengthwise into ⅛-inch-thick "noodles"
Salt
1 (24-ounce) jar gluten-free marinara sauce
1 pound ricotta cheese
¾ cup grated parmesan cheese
1 large egg
3½ tablespoons chopped fresh basil leaves, plus more for garnish
1 tablespoon Italian seasoning
Freshly ground black pepper
3 cups shredded mozzarella cheese, divided

1. Preheat the oven to 375°F. Spray a 2-quart baking dish with cooking spray.

2. In a large skillet, cook the garlic, onion, and oil over medium heat for 3 to 4 minutes, or until the garlic turns golden and the onion is fragrant. Add the ground beef and cook for about 5 minutes, or until browned and crumbled.

3. While the beef is cooking, lay the zucchini slices flat on paper towels and sprinkle with salt. Let sit for 5 minutes and then dab off any water with a new paper towel. Flip the zucchini slices over and sprinkle with salt. Dab the second side after 5 minutes, just like the first side.

4. Once the beef has fully cooked, add the marinara sauce and stir until the sauce is warm. Remove from the heat.

5. In a large bowl, combine the ricotta cheese, parmesan cheese, egg, basil, and Italian seasoning. Season with salt and pepper and mix until well combined.

continued >

6. Pour half of the meaty marinara sauce into the bottom of the prepared baking dish, followed by a flat layer of zucchini slices, half of the ricotta cheese mixture, and 1½ cups of mozzarella cheese. Repeat these layers in the same order so that the remaining 1½ cups of mozzarella cheese is the top layer.

7. Cover with aluminum foil and bake for 30 minutes. Remove the foil, increase the oven temperature to 400°F, and bake for another 10 to 15 minutes, or until the cheese is browned. Remove from the oven, sprinkle with extra basil, and let sit for 10 minutes before cutting and serving.

Prep Tip: Make sure that you prep the zucchini with the salt. If you skip this step, the lasagna will have quite a bit of liquid in the bottom.

Per serving: Calories: 802; Total Fat: 52g; Saturated Fat: 27g; Cholesterol: 265mg; Carbohydrates: 21g; Fiber: 3g; Sodium: 1,105mg; Protein: 63g

Peanut Butter
Rocky Road Bars,
page 138

CHAPTER 8

Desserts

Peach Crumble

Prep time: 10 minutes **Cook time:** 35 minutes

Crumbles are a great dessert for those who aren't detail oriented but want a beautiful and delicious outcome. As long as you can mix together the peach fruit filling, pour it into a baking dish, and top with a quick topping, you've got this deconstructed dessert covered. This crumble is also perfectly partnered with a fresh drizzle of honey or scoops of vanilla ice cream. **Serves 8**

FOR THE FRUIT FILLING

Gluten-free cooking spray, for coating the baking dish
4 fresh peaches, pitted and sliced
⅓ cup granulated sugar
⅓ cup packed light brown sugar
3 tablespoons cornstarch
1 tablespoon freshly squeezed lemon juice
1 teaspoon vanilla extract
Pinch salt

FOR THE CRUMBLE

¾ cup gluten-free oats
½ cup almond flour
⅓ cup unsalted butter, melted
⅓ cup packed light brown sugar
½ teaspoon ground cinnamon

TO MAKE THE FRUIT FILLING

1. Preheat the oven to 350°F. Grease a 9-inch square baking dish or equivalent with cooking spray.

2. In a large bowl, combine the peaches, granulated sugar, brown sugar, cornstarch, lemon juice, vanilla extract, and salt and mix well.

3. Pour the fruit filling into the prepared baking dish.

TO MAKE THE CRUMBLE

4. In a medium bowl, combine the oats, flour, butter, brown sugar, and cinnamon and mix well. Sprinkle the crumble topping on top of the fruit and spread into a thin, even layer. Bake for 30 to 35 minutes, or until the peach glaze is bubbling along the sides and the crumble is golden brown around the edge of the dish.

5. Remove from the oven and allow to cool. The juices will thicken upon cooling.

Per serving: Calories: 295; Total Fat: 11g; Saturated Fat: 4g; Cholesterol: 20mg; Carbohydrates: 47g; Fiber: 3g; Sodium: 85mg; Protein: 4g

Apple Bread Pudding

Prep time: 5 minutes **Cook time:** 1 hour

This is one of the simplest desserts you can make on one of those lazy weekend days when you are craving a sweet treat. The warm, gooey pudding uses up extra gluten-free bread you may have lying around. If you can't find butterscotch chips for this recipe, use caramel chips for a similar flavor. **Serves 10**

Gluten-free cooking spray, for coating the Dutch oven
7 cups cubed day-old gluten-free sandwich bread
4 large eggs
1 cup applesauce
¾ cup heavy cream
½ cup pecans, chopped
½ cup butterscotch chips
8 tablespoons (1 stick) unsalted butter, melted
½ cup lightly packed light brown sugar
1½ teaspoons vanilla extract
¾ teaspoon ground cinnamon
¾ teaspoon ground allspice, plus more for sprinkling

1. Preheat the oven to 225°F. Spray the inside of a Dutch oven or large oven-safe lidded stove pot with cooking spray.

2. Pour the bread cubes into the Dutch oven.

3. In a medium bowl, combine the eggs, applesauce, cream, pecans, butterscotch, butter, sugar, vanilla, cinnamon, and allspice and stir until well mixed.

4. Pour the egg mixture over the bread cubes and stir until just combined. Sprinkle with a pinch more allspice.

5. Cover the Dutch oven with its lid and bake for 55 minutes to 1 hour, or until warm, moist, and gooey. Remove from the oven and serve while warm.

Something Extra: If you are looking to add some more fruit to this dessert, try adding 1 or 2 chopped apples after the bread has been put in the Dutch oven; cook for an additional 5 minutes.

Per serving: Calories: 346; Total Fat: 23g; Saturated Fat: 11g; Cholesterol: 123mg; Carbohydrates: 32g; Fiber: 2g; Sodium: 255mg; Protein: 6g

Peanut Butter Rocky Road Bars

Prep time: 15 minutes, plus 3 hours to chill **Cook time:** 15 minutes

These bars are one of my favorite warm-weather treats. Quick and simple to put together, they don't require you to heat up the oven on a hot day. In fact, they're chilled in the refrigerator for a refreshing twist with every bite. **Makes 16 bars**

1¾ cups creamy peanut butter
1½ cups packed light brown sugar
1½ cups powdered sugar
5 tablespoons unsalted butter, melted
3 cups semisweet chocolate chips
1¼ cups gluten-free mini marshmallows
⅓ cup chopped pecans
¼ teaspoon sea salt

1. Line an 8-inch square baking pan with parchment paper.

2. In a medium bowl, stir together the peanut butter, brown sugar, powdered sugar, and butter. Mix well and press it with your fingers into an even level in the prepared baking pan.

3. In a medium microwavable bowl, heat the chocolate chips according to the package instructions.

4. Pour half of the melted chocolate over the peanut butter crust and spread evenly.

5. Sprinkle the marshmallows and pecans over the melted chocolate layer and then drizzle the remaining melted chocolate on top in a smooth layer. Sprinkle with the salt.

6. Refrigerate for 2 to 3 hours, or until firm. Cut into squares only after it is completely chilled.

Ingredient Swap: If you prefer, you can substitute creamy almond butter for the peanut butter.

Per serving (1 bar): Calories: 528; Total Fat: 32g; Saturated Fat: 12g; Cholesterol: 11mg; Carbohydrates: 56g; Fiber: 4g; Sodium: 197mg; Protein: 9g

White Chocolate Blondies

Prep time: 5 minutes **Cook time:** 25 minutes

Gluten-free blondies are all the rage in our house. We love nibbling on sweet treats that have the texture and consistency of warm, moist brownies and all the luscious flavors of bakery-style vanilla cupcakes. These squares incredibly only take about 30 minutes to make. **Makes 16 blondies**

Gluten-free cooking spray, for coating
1 cup (2 sticks) unsalted butter, melted
¾ cup packed light brown sugar
½ cup granulated sugar
2 large eggs, beaten
2 tablespoons vanilla extract
½ teaspoon salt
2 cups gluten-free baking flour blend
2 teaspoons baking powder
¾ cup white chocolate chips

1. Preheat the oven to 350°F. Line an 8-inch or 9-inch square baking pan with aluminum foil and spray with cooking spray.

2. In a large bowl, combine the butter, brown sugar, granulated sugar, eggs, vanilla, and salt and stir until completely mixed.

3. Add the flour and baking powder in ½-cup increments, stirring thoroughly between increments until a thick, consistent batter forms. Stir in the chocolate chips.

4. Pour the batter into the prepared baking dish and bake for 18 to 22 minutes, or until the edges start to turn golden brown. Do not overbake.

5. Remove from the oven and cool for 5 minutes, then transfer the blondies to a wire rack to cool completely. Cut into squares and serve.

Helpful Hack: I highly recommend Bob's Red Mill Gluten-Free 1:1 Baking Flour for this recipe. These blondies come out perfectly every time this flour blend is used. It is also one of the most affordable, accessible blends.

Per serving (1 blondie bar): Calories: 287; Total Fat: 15g; Saturated Fat: 9g; Cholesterol: 55mg; Carbohydrates: 37g; Fiber: 1g; Sodium: 189mg; Protein: 2g

Gooey S'mores

Prep time: 5 minutes, plus 30 minutes to chill **Cook time:** 20 minutes

Once I discovered how wonderful homemade gluten-free Graham crackers can taste, there was really no going back to the store-bought versions come camping and s'mores season. In fact, even my non-gluten-free friends and family request to use my s'mores ingredients over their store-bought ingredients that are full of gluten. **Makes 12 bars**

2¼ cups almond flour
½ cup packed light
   brown sugar
1 teaspoon baking powder
½ teaspoon ground
   cinnamon
½ teaspoon ground allspice
½ teaspoon fine sea salt
1 large egg, beaten
2 tablespoons honey
2 tablespoons coconut oil
Marshmallows, for assembly
24 Graham crackers
12 milk chocolate bars

1. To make the dough, in a large bowl, combine the flour, sugar, baking powder, cinnamon, allspice, and salt and mix well.

2. Add the egg, honey, and oil and stir until well combined. Put the bowl in the refrigerator for 30 minutes to chill.

3. Preheat the oven to 325°F. Line a large baking sheet with parchment paper.

4. Set the dough on the prepared baking sheet and place a second sheet of parchment paper on top of the dough.

5. Roll out the dough with a rolling pin to a ⅛- to ¼-inch thickness and cut into squares.

6. Bake for 12 to 14 minutes, or until the edges turn golden but the centers are still soft. Remove from the oven and allow to cool and harden for a few minutes on the baking sheet before transferring to a cooling rack.

7. When ready to make s'mores, heat marshmallows in the microwave for 10 to 15 seconds or over an open flame. Allow to form a golden brown crust on the outside and immediately place between 2 Graham crackers and a chocolate bar piece. Let cool for 30 to 60 seconds to allow the chocolate to melt.

- -

Cooking Technique: Make sure to not undercook the crackers. If they are not cooked enough, the centers will be too soft and won't be able to support the s'mores toppings.

- -

Per serving (1 s'more): Calories: 329; Total Fat: 18g; Saturated Fat: 8g; Cholesterol: 22mg; Carbohydrates: 38g; Fiber: 3g; Sodium: 134mg; Protein: 6g

Simple Crème Brûlée

Prep time: 15 minutes **Cook time:** 1 hour

Crème brûlée is one of my favorite desserts to order when eating out because it's almost always already gluten-free and, best of all, simply tastes amazing. That creamy, thick custard coated with a caramelized golden brown crust is hard to resist. With only five ingredients, you can easily start making crème brûlée at home so you don't have to wait until the next date night out to get your favorite dessert fix. You can use 6-, 7-, or 8-ounce ramekins for this recipe. **Serves 6**

4 cups heavy cream
1½ teaspoons vanilla extract
1 cup sugar, divided
6 large egg yolks
8 cups hot water

1. Preheat the oven to 325°F.

2. In a medium pan, combine the cream and vanilla and bring to a boil over medium-high heat. Remove from the heat, cover the pan, and allow to cool for 10 to 15 minutes.

3. In a bowl, whisk together ½ cup of sugar and the egg yolks. Blend well. Add the cream mixture a little bit at a time, stirring continuously.

4. Put 6 ramekins in a baking pan and then pour the liquid mixture into the ramekins.

5. Pour the hot water into the baking pan to reach halfway up the sides of the ramekins. Carefully slide the baking pan into the oven and bake for 40 to 45 minutes, or until the mixture is just starting to set (it will still be jiggly in the center). Remove from the oven.

6. Refrigerate the ramekins for at least 3 hours. Remove from the refrigerator 30 minutes before serving. Divide the remaining ½ cup of sugar on top of the 6 ramekins and smooth the surface of each.

7. Using a torch, crystalize the sugar until it turns an amber-golden brown. Allow a few minutes to cool before serving.

Cooking Technique: It is important to use a 6- to 8-ounce ramekin for this recipe. Too big or too small a dish will impact the final product, and it will likely not set up correctly.

Per serving: Calories: 734; Total Fat: 63g; Saturated Fat: 38g; Cholesterol: 402mg; Carbohydrates: 39g; Fiber: 0g; Sodium: 69mg; Protein: 6g

Easy Sugar Cookies

Prep time: 10 minutes, plus 3 hours to chill **Cook time:** 15 minutes

One of the treats that I missed most when I first started out on my gluten-free journey were simple sugar cookies. I have spent more than 10 years perfecting this recipe for moist and soft sugar cookies. These are awesome on their own, sprinkled with a touch of coarse sugar, or topped with a thick swipe of vanilla frosting with sprinkles. They will keep well refrigerated in an airtight container for up to 7 days. **Makes 12 cookies**

½ cup sugar
8 tablespoons (1 stick) unsalted butter, at room temperature
½ large egg, beaten
½ tablespoon milk of choice
½ teaspoon vanilla extract
¾ cup white rice flour, plus more as needed
¼ cup potato starch
¼ cup tapioca flour
2 teaspoons xanthan gum
½ teaspoon baking powder
⅛ teaspoon salt

1. In a mixer, beat the sugar and butter together until smooth; use a large bowl if using a hand mixer. Add the egg, milk, and vanilla and mix until smooth. In a large bowl, combine the rice flour, potato starch, tapioca flour, xanthan gum, baking powder, and salt and stir until well combined.

2. Slowly add the flour mixture to the wet ingredients, keeping the mixer on low speed throughout, until all the flour mix is well blended and a homogenous dough has formed. If the dough is still sticking to the sides of the bowl, add more rice flour 1 tablespoon at a time to the dough until it no longer sticks.

3. Wrap the dough ball in plastic wrap and place in the refrigerator to chill for 1½ to 3 hours.

4. Preheat the oven to 375°F. Line a baking sheet with parchment paper.

5. Roll the dough into golf ball–size balls with your hands. Place the dough balls on the prepared baking sheet, 2 inches apart from one another. Using the palm of your hand, press down on each dough ball so that they are all about ½ inch thick.

6. Bake on the middle rack for 11 to 13 minutes, or until the edges of the cookies start to turn golden brown. Remove from the oven to cool for 5 minutes before transferring to a cooling rack to cool further.

Per serving (1 cookie): Calories: 161; Total Fat: 8g; Saturated Fat: 5g; Cholesterol: 28mg; Carbohydrates: 21g; Fiber: 1g; Sodium: 92mg; Protein: 1g

Decadent Chocolate Cake

Prep time: 40 minutes **Cook time:** 40 minutes

Gluten-free chocolate cake with homemade chocolate frosting is the ultimate in chocolate decadence. It is also easy enough for a beginner cook to create, yet it tastes like a professional baker came into your kitchen and baked it. This cake is the perfect homemade gift idea for any chocolate lover in your life. **Serves 12**

FOR THE CAKE

Gluten-free cooking spray, for coating the pan

1¾ cups gluten-free Bisquick mix or Homemade Gluten-Free Baking Mix (page 13)

1½ cups sugar

¾ cup baking cocoa powder

½ teaspoon salt

¼ teaspoon baking powder

¼ teaspoon baking soda

2 large eggs, beaten

1 cup milk

½ cup canola oil

1½ tablespoons vanilla extract

¾ cup boiling water

FOR THE FROSTING

1½ cups (3 sticks) unsalted butter, at room temperature

5 to 7 tablespoons milk

3 cups powdered sugar

1 cup very dark cocoa powder

¼ cup melted dark chocolate

TO MAKE THE CAKE

1. Preheat the oven to 350°F. Generously spray a 9-inch round or square baking pan with cooking spray.

2. In a large bowl, combine the baking mix, sugar, cocoa powder, salt, baking powder, and baking soda and mix well. Add the eggs, milk, oil, and vanilla and stir until well combined. Pour in the water, ¼ cup at a time, while constantly stirring.

3. Pour the batter evenly into the prepared baking pan. Bake for 35 to 38 minutes, or until a toothpick inserted into the center comes out clean.

4. Remove the cake from the oven and set on a wire rack (still in the pan) to cool for 10 minutes. Remove from the pan and let the cake cool to room temperature.

5. Beat the butter until smooth. Add the milk and combine again. Slowly add the powdered sugar and cocoa powder until combined. Add the melted chocolate and combine for another 2 minutes, or until it reaches a thick frosting consistency.

6. Frost the cake once it has fully cooled to room temperature.

Something Extra: If this cake isn't decadent enough for you as it stands, I highly recommend adding fresh seasonal berries on top for the most amazing garnish and an added splash of sweetness. Try strawberries, raspberries, blackberries, or blueberries.

Per serving: Calories: 623; Total Fat: 37g; Saturated Fat: 17g; Cholesterol: 95mg; Carbohydrates: 73g; Fiber: 4g; Sodium: 504mg; Protein: 6g

Double Chocolate Brownies

Prep time: 10 minutes **Cook time:** 40 minutes

If brownies aren't deeply chocolaty, decadently moist, perfectly smooth, and sweet, then they just aren't worth eating. This brownie recipe is totally worth the minimal effort it takes you to make. You won't find a recipe for a moister, softer, more irresistible gluten-free brownie anywhere.

Makes 16 brownies

1 cup granulated sugar

12 tablespoons (1½ sticks) unsalted butter, melted

½ cup packed light brown sugar

1½ teaspoons vanilla extract

3 large eggs

½ cup cocoa powder

¼ cup tapioca flour

¼ cup brown rice flour

1 tablespoon xanthan gum

½ cup chocolate chips

¼ teaspoon sea salt

1. Preheat the oven to 350°F. Line an 8-inch square baking pan with parchment paper.

2. In a large bowl, combine the granulated sugar, butter, brown sugar, and vanilla and mix well. Add the eggs and stir until well combined and smooth. Add the cocoa powder and stir until well combined. Add the tapioca flour, rice flour, and xanthan gum and stir until a smooth batter forms. Fold in the chocolate chips.

3. Pour the batter into the prepared baking pan in an even layer. Sprinkle with the salt and bake on the middle rack for 35 to 40 minutes, or until the outer edges become darker and harder to the touch and a toothpick inserted into the center of the brownies comes out clean.

4. Remove from the oven and cool to room temperature in the pan.

5. When ready to serve, cut into 16 squares and enjoy. Store leftovers in an airtight container for up to 5 days.

- -

Per serving (1 brownie): Calories: 211; Total Fat: 12g; Saturated Fat: 7g; Cholesterol: 58mg; Carbohydrates: 27g; Fiber: 1g; Sodium: 121mg; Protein: 2g

Vanilla Cupcakes

Prep time: 10 minutes **Cook time:** 25 minutes

Never again do you have to opt out of a celebratory cupcake. Now that you have this recipe for classic vanilla cupcakes that you can make at home, your friends and family who are lucky enough to taste these will always be asking for this version. **Makes 24 cupcakes**

FOR THE CUPCAKES

1½ cups sugar
1 cup white rice flour
½ cup brown rice flour
½ cup potato starch
¼ cup tapioca flour
1 tablespoon baking powder
2 teaspoons xanthan gum
¾ teaspoon salt
3 large eggs
¾ cup milk
12 tablespoons (1½ sticks) unsalted butter, at room temperature
2 tablespoons almond extract

FOR THE FROSTING

8 tablespoons (1 stick) unsalted butter, at room temperature
2 cups powdered sugar
½ teaspoon vanilla extract
2½ tablespoons heavy cream

TO MAKE THE CUPCAKES

1. Preheat the oven to 350°F. Line a regular muffin tin with cupcake liners.

2. In a large bowl, combine the sugar, white rice flour, brown rice flour, potato starch, tapioca flour, baking powder, xanthan gum, and salt and mix well. Add the eggs, milk, butter, and almond extract and stir until well combined and a smooth batter forms.

3. Pour the batter into the cupcake liners until two-thirds full. Bake on the middle rack for 20 to 23 minutes, or until the tops are golden brown and a toothpick inserted into the center of a cupcake comes out clean. Remove from the oven and cool to room temperature in the muffin tin.

TO MAKE THE FROSTING

4. In a large bowl, mix together the butter and powdered sugar. Add the vanilla and cream and stir until smooth and well combined. Frost the cupcakes when cool, then serve.

- -

Per serving (1 cupcake): Calories: 238; Total Fat: 11g; Saturated Fat: 6g; Cholesterol: 52mg; Carbohydrates: 33g; Fiber: 1g; Sodium: 164mg; Protein: 2g

Caesar Dressing, page 157

CHAPTER 9

Dips, Dressings, and Sauces

Sour Cream–Feta Dip

Prep time: 5 minutes

Light and creamy feta dip is an addictive appetizer that welcomes just about anything as a dipper. This version has no cream cheese in it. Instead, I use sour cream, which makes this dish smoother and adds to the savory notes. This is pretty when drizzled with a little olive oil and garnished with lemon zest. **Serves 6**

8 ounces feta cheese crumbles

1 tablespoon minced garlic

1 cup sour cream

2 tablespoons freshly squeezed lemon juice

⅛ teaspoon red pepper flakes

⅛ teaspoon salt

⅛ teaspoon freshly ground black pepper

1. In a food processor, pulse the cheese until finely grated.

2. Pour the cheese into a medium bowl. Add the garlic, sour cream, lemon juice, red pepper flakes, salt, and pepper and stir until well combined and smooth.

Ingredient Swap: You can substitute mayonnaise or Greek yogurt for the sour cream.

Per serving: Calories: 177; Total Fat: 16g; Saturated Fat: 10g; Cholesterol: 54mg; Carbohydrates: 3g; Fiber: 0g; Sodium: 417mg; Protein: 6g

ONE POT, 30 MINUTES OR LESS, NUT-FREE, LOW-CARB, VEGETARIAN

Spinach-Artichoke Dip

Prep time: 5 minutes **Cook time:** 10 minutes

There's something about the layers of different cheeses, the textures of the vegetables, and the combination of spices that make this dip irresistible. We like to mix it up in my house; sometimes we use this dip with chips, sometimes with vegetable sticks or spears, and sometimes spooned over grilled or baked chicken. This classic dip is one of the most requested dips that I make. **Serves 6**

1 tablespoon olive oil

2 tablespoons minced garlic

4 cups fresh spinach

1 (8-ounce) brick cream cheese

½ cup sour cream

1 cup shredded mozzarella cheese

¾ cup shredded parmesan cheese

1 (14-ounce) jar artichokes, drained and coarsely chopped

¼ teaspoon paprika

¼ teaspoon salt

¼ teaspoon freshly ground black pepper

1. In a large skillet, heat the oil over low heat for 2 to 3 minutes. Add the garlic and cook for 2 minutes, or until fragrant. Add the spinach and cook, stirring occasionally, for 3 to 4 minutes, or until all the leaves are wilted.

2. Add the cream cheese, sour cream, mozzarella, cheese, and parmesan cheese and stir until all the cheese is melted. Add the artichokes, paprika, salt, and pepper and stir until well combined.

3. Remove from the heat and pour into a serving bowl. Serve while still warm.

Ingredient Swap: Try substituting gluten-free mayonnaise or plain Greek yogurt for the sour cream. Dip with veggie sticks, chips, crackers, or gluten-free toast pieces (see Quick Al Fresco Bruschetta on page 53).

Per serving: Calories: 329; Total Fat: 27g; Saturated Fat: 14g; Cholesterol: 77mg; Carbohydrates: 12g; Fiber: 5g; Sodium: 631mg; Protein: 12g

Quick Queso Dip

Prep time: 5 minutes **Cook time:** 10 minutes

It takes just a few minutes to put together this quick queso dip, and everyone loves it. Try this dip with Crispy Tortilla Chips (page 44), crackers, vegetable pieces, or spooned over cooked chicken pieces as a complement to the main course. It is a party favorite. **Serves 6 to 8**

2 tablespoons unsalted butter
½ cup chopped sweet onion
1 tablespoon minced garlic
1 (10-ounce) can Rotel tomatoes
1 (14½-ounce) can diced tomatoes
¾ teaspoon ground cumin
½ teaspoon salt
½ teaspoon chili powder
¼ teaspoon cayenne pepper
1 (12-ounce) can evaporated milk
8 to 12 ounces shredded Cheddar cheese

1. In a large nonstick skillet, melt the butter over medium heat. Add the onion and garlic and cook for 3 to 4 minutes, or until fragrant, translucent, and tender.

2. Add the Rotel tomatoes, diced tomatoes, cumin, salt, chili powder, and cayenne. Stir, bring to a simmer, and cook for 5 minutes.

3. Add the evaporated milk and cheese. Stir until the cheese is melted. Remove from the heat. Serve while warm.

Prep Tip: If you prefer thicker dip, use closer to 12 ounces shredded Cheddar cheese; if you like a thinner dip, stick to 8 ounces and add more until the desired consistency is reached.

Per serving: Calories: 269; Total Fat: 17g; Saturated Fat: 10g; Cholesterol: 51mg; Carbohydrates: 15g; Fiber: 3g; Sodium: 709mg; Protein: 15g

Adobo Barbecue Sauce

Prep time: 5 minutes

This is a thick, dark sauce that is a bit tangy and a lot savory. The natural spice of the peppers means you can customize the heat for all different types of palates. This sauce can be whipped up in minutes but will be raved about for hours. **Makes 1 cup**

1 (7-ounce) can chipotle
    peppers in adobo sauce
½ cup honey
1 teaspoon garlic powder
1 teaspoon dried oregano
½ teaspoon ground allspice

Pour the can of chipotle peppers in adobo sauce into a food processor and pulse until the peppers are finely diced and the sauce has turned into a dark-red paste. Stir in the honey, garlic powder, oregano, and allspice until well combined.

Cooking Technique: If spice isn't your thing, remove the actual peppers from the adobo sauce before putting the ingredients in the food processor and blending. The peppers are what bring the heat.

Per serving (2 tablespoons): Calories: 72; Total Fat: 0g; Saturated Fat: 0g; Cholesterol: 0mg; Carbohydrates: 19g; Fiber: 1g; Sodium: 292mg; Protein: 0g

Poppy Seed Dressing

Prep time: 5 minutes

This tangy and sweet dressing gets its creamy base from Greek yogurt. A creamy dressing that is still light and refreshing, it is perfect for almost any salad. This dressing is also great as a marinade for chicken or as a dip for all kinds of snacks and appetizers. Store this dressing in an airtight container in the refrigerator for up to 5 days. **Makes 1⅓ cups**

⅓ cup distilled white vinegar
¼ cup maple syrup
⅛ teaspoon salt
½ teaspoon minced garlic
½ cup olive oil
¼ cup Greek yogurt
1 tablespoon poppy seeds

In a blender, combine the vinegar, maple syrup, salt, garlic, oil, and yogurt and blend until thoroughly combined. Stir in the poppy seeds.

Cooking Technique: Do not stir the poppy seeds into the dressing until after all the other ingredients have been well blended in order to keep the poppy seeds whole and crunchy.

Per serving (2 tablespoons): Calories: 126; Total Fat: 11g; Saturated Fat: 2g; Cholesterol: 1mg; Carbohydrates: 6g; Fiber: 0g; Sodium: 35mg; Protein: 0g

Caesar Dressing

Prep time: 5 minutes

A good Caesar dressing is both hearty in its creaminess and light in its lemony zest. This homemade version is not only delicious but also incredibly simple and fast to put together. So, if you need a salad dressing but don't have the time to run to the store, give this a try. **Serves 2**

¼ cup gluten-free
  mayonnaise
⅓ cup grated parmesan
  cheese
2 tablespoons olive oil
1½ tablespoons freshly
  squeezed lemon juice
1½ teaspoons Dijon mustard
1 teaspoon anchovy paste
2 garlic cloves
⅛ teaspoon freshly ground
  black pepper

In a food processor, combine the mayonnaise, cheese, oil, lemon juice, mustard, anchovy paste, garlic, and pepper. Blend until smooth. Refrigerate until ready to use. Store leftovers in an airtight container in the refrigerator for up to 5 days.

Cooking Technique: If you like Caesar dressing a little bit on the thicker side, use 1 to 2 tablespoons less mayonnaise, and if you like it a little thinner, add 1 to 2 extra tablespoons olive oil.

Per serving: Calories: 576; Total Fat: 60g; Saturated Fat: 11g; Cholesterol: 39mg; Carbohydrates: 5g; Fiber: 0g; Sodium: 763mg; Protein: 6g

Buffalo Chicken Dip

Prep time: 5 minutes **Cook time:** 15 minutes

Snacking on Buffalo chicken is always a great idea, but when it is turned into a dip, taste buds celebrate. My family treats this recipe as a dip with homemade Crispy Tortilla Chips (page 44), and we also love it on top of grilled or roasted chicken breasts. It is a great option for making ahead of time and keeping in the refrigerator until ready to serve. Then just warm it in the microwave for 45 to 60 seconds. **Serves 6 to 8**

8 ounces cream cheese, cubed

1 cup plain nonfat Greek yogurt or gluten-free mayonnaise or sour cream

1 cup hot sauce (Frank's RedHot is great)

1 teaspoon freshly ground black pepper

1 teaspoon garlic powder

2 (10-ounce) cans chicken, drained and shredded

½ cup chopped scallions, green parts only

1½ cups shredded mozzarella cheese, divided

2 cups shredded Cheddar cheese, divided

1. Preheat the oven to 350°F.

2. In a large oven-safe nonstick skillet, combine the cream cheese, yogurt, hot sauce, pepper, and garlic powder and heat over medium heat, stirring, until the cheese is melted.

3. Add the chicken, scallions, 1 cup of mozzarella cheese, and 1½ cups of Cheddar cheese and stir until all the cheese is melted.

4. Top the skillet with the remaining ½ cup of mozzarella cheese and ½ cup of Cheddar cheese and bake for 5 to 10 minutes, or until the cheese has melted completely. Remove from the oven and cool for 3 to 5 minutes before serving.

Per serving: Calories: 475; Total Fat: 36g; Saturated Fat: 19g; Cholesterol: 125mg; Carbohydrates: 6g; Fiber: 1g; Sodium: 915mg; Protein: 33g

ONE POT, 30 MINUTES OR LESS, NUT-FREE, VEGETARIAN

French Onion Dip

Prep time: 5 minutes **Cook time:** 25 minutes

Dips that are just as good chilled as they are served warm cannot be beat. This French onion dip is just that. If you like the dip warm, serve it right out of the skillet. If you prefer it at room temperature or chilled, it's equally good. This tangy, garlicky, and perfectly onion-y concoction will be gone in minutes, no matter which way you serve it up. **Serves 6 to 8**

3 tablespoons unsalted butter

1 large sweet onion, diced

1 teaspoon garlic powder

½ teaspoon salt

½ teaspoon freshly ground
   black pepper

4 ounces cream cheese

½ cup sour cream

¼ cup gluten-free
   mayonnaise

1. In a large nonstick skillet, melt the butter over medium heat. Add the onion and cook for 3 to 4 minutes, or until fragrant, translucent, and tender.

2. Add the garlic powder, salt, and pepper, stir, and reduce the heat to medium-low. Allow the onion to caramelize and cook for an additional 20 minutes, stirring occasionally.

3. Add the cream cheese, sour cream, and mayonnaise and stir until all is melted and well combined. Remove from the heat and serve warm, or cool to room temperature, refrigerate in an airtight container for 1 to 2 hours, and serve chilled.

Prep Tip: For a bit of spicy heat, try sprinkling in ¼ teaspoon cayenne pepper with the other seasoning when caramelizing the onions.

Per serving: Calories: 234; Total Fat: 23g; Saturated Fat: 11g; Cholesterol: 50mg; Carbohydrates: 6g; Fiber: 1g; Sodium: 380mg; Protein: 2g

Teriyaki Sauce

Prep time: 5 minutes **Cook time:** 20 minutes

Teriyaki sauce is part of many Asian-inspired dishes. However, there are few gluten-free teriyaki sauces out there that really stand out. That's why I recommend whipping this recipe up. It's quick and easy, and you will notice a huge difference in quality between this homemade sauce and any bottle of store-bought sauce. You'll be hooked. **Makes 1½ to 2 cups**

1 cup water, plus
   2 tablespoons
⅓ cup gluten-free soy sauce
   or soy or coconut aminos
5 tablespoons packed light
   brown sugar
1 tablespoon minced garlic
½ teaspoon ground ginger
2 tablespoons cornstarch

1. In a medium saucepan, combine 1 cup of water, the soy sauce, sugar, garlic, and ginger over medium heat. Simmer, stirring occasionally, for 10 to 15 minutes.

2. Meanwhile, in a small bowl, combine the remaining 2 tablespoons of water and the cornstarch and mix very well to form a slurry.

3. Whisk in the slurry and allow the sauce to return to a simmer. Cook for an additional 5 minutes.

4. Remove from the heat and allow to sit for 5 minutes before serving.

Prep Tip: If you like a spicy teriyaki, add ½ to 1 tablespoon red pepper flakes to the sauce during the final 5 minutes of simmering. You may also sprinkle sesame seeds into the dish at the same time for a little extra pizazz.

Per serving (¼ cup): Calories: 49; Total Fat: 0g; Saturated Fat: 0g; Cholesterol: 0mg; Carbohydrates: 11g; Fiber: 0g; Sodium: 508mg; Protein: 1g

Creamy Alfredo Sauce

Prep time: 5 minutes **Cook time:** 10 minutes

Alfredo sauce is great on top of your favorite pasta, drizzled on pizza or flatbread, mixed in with casserole fixings, spread on roasted chicken, or as the best dip ever. This specific recipe is incredibly rich with garlic, cream, and cheeses. Top it off with black pepper and chopped basil to take any dish over the top and all in only 15 minutes. **Makes 2 to 2½ cups**

2 cups heavy cream
8 tablespoons (1 stick) unsalted butter
4 ounces cream cheese
1 cup grated parmesan cheese
2 teaspoons garlic powder
2 teaspoons Italian seasoning
1 teaspoon minced garlic
¼ teaspoon salt
½ teaspoon freshly ground black pepper
Chopped fresh basil leaves, for garnish (optional)

1. In a medium or large skillet, heat the cream, butter, and cream cheese over medium heat until the butter is melted. Add the parmesan cheese, garlic powder, Italian seasoning, garlic, salt, and pepper and stir to combine. Simmer for 5 to 10 minutes, or until the sauce thickens to your liking.

2. Remove from the heat and allow to cool for 3 to 4 minutes before serving. Serve sprinkled with basil (if using).

Cooking Technique: Do not cook this sauce on too high a temperature. A light simmer is all it needs to make a perfect, thick sauce. Too high a temperature may cause uneven consistency of the sauce.

Per serving (¼ cup): Calories: 411; Total Fat: 42g; Saturated Fat: 27g; Cholesterol: 138mg; Carbohydrates: 5g; Fiber: 0g; Sodium: 464mg; Protein: 6g

Enchilada Sauce

Prep time: 5 minutes **Cook time:** 20 minutes

This homemade version of enchilada sauce has no hidden gluten, unlike many enchilada sauces available in the grocery store. Instead, the combination of spices and broth balances out to a mild enchilada sauce that can be used for any Mexican-inspired dish that you'd like. **Makes 2 to 2½ cups**

2 tablespoons olive oil

2 tablespoons white rice flour

4½ tablespoons chili powder

1 tablespoon garlic powder

½ teaspoon salt

½ teaspoon ground cumin

½ teaspoon dried oregano

2 cups vegetable broth

1. In a medium saucepan, heat the oil over medium-high heat for 1 to 2 minutes. Add the flour and continuously stir for 30 seconds, or until all the liquid is absorbed.

2. Stir in the chili powder, garlic powder, salt, cumin, and oregano, then immediately whisk in the broth until well combined.

3. Bring the sauce to a boil and, stirring occasionally, cook for 12 to 15 minutes, or until the sauce is slightly thickened and reduced by about one-fourth. Remove from the heat and allow to cool for 3 to 5 minutes before using.

4. Store room-temperature leftover sauce in an airtight container in the refrigerator for up to 5 days.

- -

Prep Tip: If you want to add extra spice to this mild sauce, you can build up the spice to your preferred heat level, but add the extra heat at the end once the sauce is done cooking. A pinch of cayenne pepper will likely do the trick.

- -

Per serving (¼ cup): Calories: 59; Total Fat: 4g; Saturated Fat: 1g; Cholesterol: 0mg; Carbohydrates: 6g; Fiber: 2g; Sodium: 413mg; Protein: 1g

ONE POT, 30 MINUTES OR LESS, NUT-FREE, LOW-CARB, VEGAN

Greek Vinaigrette

Prep time: 5 minutes

Light, crisp, and refreshing, this Greek dressing takes just a few minutes to whip together with simple ingredients from your kitchen. Use this dressing for salads, pasta salads, or as a marinade for your favorite proteins.

Serves 4 to 6

¼ cup olive oil
2½ tablespoons freshly
   squeezed lemon juice
2 tablespoons red-wine
   vinegar
1 tablespoon minced garlic
1 teaspoon dried oregano
½ teaspoon Italian seasoning
¼ teaspoon salt
¼ teaspoon freshly ground
   black pepper

In a medium, airtight container, combine the oil, lemon juice, vinegar, garlic, oregano, Italian seasoning, salt, and pepper and mix well. Store in the refrigerator until ready to serve. It will keep refrigerated for up to 7 days.

Prep Tip: This dressing is a great one to double or triple to make large Greek salads for parties or to use as a marinade for steak or chicken dishes.

Per serving: Calories: 127; Total Fat: 14g; Saturated Fat: 2g; Cholesterol: 0mg; Carbohydrates: 2g; Fiber: 0g; Sodium: 147mg; Protein: 0g

Honey-Mustard Dressing

Prep time: 5 minutes

Kids and adults alike can't stay away from a good honey-mustard dressing. This version is not only spectacular drizzled on fresh greens but also makes for one incredibly tasty and easy dip for foods such as Chicken Nuggets (page 114) and Mini Corn Dogs (page 58). You can also turn this dressing into a creamy honey-mustard dip by adding another ½ cup plain Greek yogurt. **Serves 4 to 6**

2½ tablespoons freshly
  squeezed lemon juice
1 tablespoon apple
  cider vinegar
2½ tablespoons honey
2½ tablespoons
  Dijon mustard
½ teaspoon minced garlic
¼ teaspoon sea salt
¼ teaspoon freshly
  ground pepper
¼ cup plain Greek yogurt

In an airtight container, combine the lemon juice, vinegar, honey, mustard, garlic, salt, pepper, and yogurt and mix well. Store in the refrigerator until ready to serve. It will keep refrigerated for up to 7 days.

Per serving: Calories: 58; Total Fat: 1g; Saturated Fat: 0g; Cholesterol: 2mg; Carbohydrates: 13g; Fiber: 1g; Sodium: 261mg; Protein: 1g

Measurement Conversions

Volume Equivalents	U.S. Standard	U.S. Standard (ounces)	Metric (approximate)
Liquid	2 tablespoons	1 fl. oz.	30 mL
	¼ cup	2 fl. oz.	60 mL
	½ cup	4 fl. oz.	120 mL
	1 cup	8 fl. oz.	240 mL
	1½ cups	12 fl. oz.	355 mL
	2 cups or 1 pint	16 fl. oz.	475 mL
	4 cups or 1 quart	32 fl. oz.	1 L
	1 gallon	128 fl. oz.	4 L
Dry	⅛ teaspoon		0.5 mL
	¼ teaspoon		1 mL
	½ teaspoon		2 mL
	¾ teaspoon		4 mL
	1 teaspoon		5 mL
	1 tablespoon		15 mL
	¼ cup		59 mL
	⅓ cup		79 mL
	½ cup		118 mL
	⅔ cup		156 mL
	¾ cup		177 mL
	1 cup		235 mL
	2 cups or 1 pint		475 mL
	3 cups		700 mL
	4 cups or 1 quart		1 L
	½ gallon		2 L
	1 gallon		4 L

Oven Temperatures

Fahrenheit	Celsius (approximate)
250°F	120°C
300°F	150°C
325°F	165°C
350°F	180°C
375°F	190°C
400°F	200°C
425°F	220°C
450°F	230°C

Weight Equivalents

U.S. Standard	Metric (approximate)
½ ounce	15 g
1 ounce	30 g
2 ounces	60 g
4 ounces	115 g
8 ounces	225 g
12 ounces	340 g
16 ounces or 1 pound	455 g

Index

Acknowledgments

I would like to thank my family and friends for their incredible support through my book publishing process. I only achieved this success because of my loving tribe. I would like to thank Julie Kirk and Tai Anderson for their enthusiasm in their roles as research assistants, especially in the pivotal areas of taste-testing and dish cleaning. Bless your hearts! Lastly, thank you to everyone who has read a post, shared a photo, bought a book, cooked through a recipe, or trusted me enough that you went out and spent your own hard-earned money on this book. I appreciate you all.

About the Author

Jessica Kirk, DVM, is an outdoor-, food-, and wine-loving extrovert. By day, she is a veterinarian in academia. By night, she teaches others how to easily cook gluten-free in their own kitchens through her website BlessHerHeartYall.com. She lives in Roswell, Georgia, with her family; two Boston terriers, Pippy and Thelma; and her horse, Scuba.

Printed in the USA
CPSIA information can be obtained
at www.ICGtesting.com
LVHW061814171223
766454LV00002B/11

9 781648 765049